Return
to the River

DAVE PELZER

#1 Worldwide Bestselling Author of *A Child Called "It"*

Return to the River

Reflections on Life Choices During a Pandemic

Health Communications, Inc.
Boca Raton, Florida

www.hcibooks.com

This is a memoir, a work of creative nonfiction. The events are portrayed to the best of Dave Pelzer's ability. While all the stories in this book are true, some names and identifying details have been changed to protect the privacy of the people involved.

**Library of Congress Cataloging-in-Publication Data
is available through the Library of Congress**

© 2023 Dave Pelzer

ISBN-13: 978-07573-2454-3 (Paperback)
ISBN-10: 07573-2454-1 (Paperback)
ISBN-13: 978-07573-2455-0 (ePub)
ISBN-10: 0-7573-2455-X (ePub)

HCI, its logos, and marks are trademarks of Health Communications, Inc.

Publisher: Health Communications, Inc.
301 Crawford Blvd., Suite 200
Boca Raton, FL 33432-3762

Cover Illustration by Nan Still
Cover, interior design and formatting by Larissa Hise Henoch

To my beautiful grandson, S. J.

Live long. And prosper. Become one with the Force, so the Force will always be with you. Be happy. Be happy now. Be good in all things. Reach out and step up to the great beyond. And when feeling down, look up in the sky . . . up, up, and away.

You've made me laugh, given me untold joy, and reconnected me in ways I can never express. As the saying goes from Hook, *one of your father's and my favorite movies when he was young: "to live will be an awfully big adventure."*

To my executive director, Kathryn Estey, "Mrs. C," my longest relationship with a woman that hasn't ended in death or divorce. In our nearly twenty years together, we've attempted to do our duty for God, country, and the world-at-large. I miss our coffee times.

To my Privilege of Youth *brother Paul Brazell, the smartest person I've ever known.*

Lastly, to "B," I do hope you are most happy. "A & F."

CONTENTS

ACKNOWLEDGMENTS

TO THE ENTIRE STAFF at Northwood Restaurant of Monte Rio, for allowing me to come in rain or shine before hours of operation and take up space at your tiny circular table longer than I should have—I am most appreciative.

To the following ladies who were extremely kind enough to take the time, chapter by chapter, to read, then take deep-felt energy to provide heart-filled feedback on the book and how it touched their own life journeys: Faviola Aguilar; Jennifer Branaman; Renee Combes, "The Mother of Monte Rio"; and Rebecca Jo Hodge. Thank you, ladies!

As always, a special nod to the book's playlist that inspired me while I wrote. First and foremost, for over twenty-five years, I've had the privilege to absorb and somehow tie-in the stirring music of Pat Metheny. In this case, the lead songs are "Polskie Drogi" and "Spiritual." Other pieces include Enya's "Drifting" and, lastly, the instrumental string version of John Barry's "We Have All the Time in the World."

A heartfelt thank-you to Nan Still for creating such a beautiful, breathtaking, nostalgic cover of the summer of '66, my most precious time with my family.

To the publishing company, Health Communications, it is nice to return. A respectful nod to the founder Mr. Peter Vegso. I wish to also acknowledge Christian Blonshine, executive vice president, for his kindness and professionalism. A shout-out to the lovable Lindsey March for her PR work. A thank-you to Bob Land for his meticulous line editing and to Christine Belleris for taking the baton most graciously and bringing this book over the finish line. Big hugs to Candace Johnson for her very extensive evaluation and suggestions that, as painful as they were for me, made the book far superior than I imagined. To my new friend for life, Allison Janse, "project manager extraordinaire," for your genuine sincerity, extreme patience, and gentle guidance. I could have never completed this Everest-like task without you!

Lastly and most importantly, to the original cheerleader of *A Child Called "It,"* Lori Golden. You are the most unpretentious person I've ever know known and are truly an angelic spirit that is a blessing to us all.

AUTHOR'S NOTE

THIS PROJECT WAS TOTALLY UNPLANNED. It literally came out of the blue. It was my fastest yet deepest writing to date. Being a hopeless romantic, part of this book is a haunting love story on various levels, with many threads. It is a story of an unexpected, overwhelming chain of events that, for me, required deep introspection on how I came to a crossroads in my later years.

Within the book is a spiritual journey about how one can be damaged yet redeemable.

It is a self-help book of sorts with the message that no matter what is happening in the world around us, within the confines of our heart, where no one else can see, we are all human. That we falter. That we fall facedown, and that at times we may lack the will to get back up, afraid to endure yet another blow.

It is a story about the circle of life. That we have to rise. We must face ourselves and our challenges. That we can only do as best we can. That we learn. That we strive to become better. And above all things, that we are all worthy and deserve happiness until the end of our days.

I thank you for taking this journey.

I truly hope it makes an impact on your inner heart and leads to a more fulfilling life.

Chapter One
THE DEEPEST OF WELLS

LATE DECEMBER 2020,
MONTE RIO—RUSSIAN RIVER, CALIFORNIA—

STANDING OUTSIDE, I'M FREEZING. Even with thick gloves the tips of my fingers are numb. My upper body quit shaking minutes ago. As much as I pace to retain heat, I can feel my body beginning to tense up and shut down. It's only a matter of time. My lower back stiffens, and the deepened calluses on both feet are beyond excruciating.

I've fought for years to bury so much in too many areas and at infinite levels. And now I feel exposed. I can't hide things as well as I used to. In the past two years, unexpected events have burst my "hurt lockers" wide open.

I'm a master of masking in plain sight. I had to learn to do so before kindergarten. I've buried so much for decades upon decades—insecurity, unworthiness, chasing others' approval, the fear of not being good enough, and above all, the dread of abandonment. As of late, I feel from deep within, in order to try to keep my hypersonic life from spinning out of orbit; in the middle of COVID World, my mask is overt. On the outside, my eyes smile, but behind the cloth, where no one can see, with every step my internal pain is beyond anything I've ever experienced.

For me, it's never about the physical pain; that I can take. That I can switch off—or at least, used to. As I became older, I seemed to have little to no control over the psychological fallout from my past.

I haven't felt this intense freezing-like sensation since I was a child, surviving in the basement that was used as a garage as Mother's secret, enslaved prisoner.

The only thing that keeps me from submitting is my private trigger. My very own deeply embedded molten resentment against myself.

And yet, today of all days, I crave positive human connection. Any connection. That no matter how bloody, disgusting, hard-charging, into-harm's-way my lifestyle may be, today I need to believe that I've accomplished something that mattered. Some minuscule thing that can relieve someone else's pain. It would go a long way to help me feel cleaner.

Behind all my layers, I long to feel cleansed.

On the outside, I am overly kind and courteous. I have a quick, razor-sharp wit and enjoy making others burst out in laughter from an unexpected joke, even when I'm under extreme duress. Of all things, I pride myself in being of service to others.

I have my reasons.

Yet today, deep within my hidden bunker-core, I feel disgusted with myself. I've unexpectedly become lost. I feel thrown away as if I were radioactive garbage. My heart is completely shattered. I had completely lowered my guard, and now I am beyond broken.

Today, I'm sixty.

Unlike those who have regaled me with celebratory stories of cruise-ship adventures or trips to high-end wineries, for the past three birthdays I've chosen a different path.

Even while mourning two unexpected losses, and as painfully crushed as I am, I fully realize how damn lucky I am. The mind-blowing adventures I've been allowed to experience are straight out of a meshed version of James Bond meets *Mission Impossible* meets Jack Bauer from the series *24*.

Or how I've always been phenomenally blessed. How many—so many—people I've barely known, folks I've never met, have prayed for me. Or how my cherished son, Stephen, whom I named after my father, and his wife, Cyndel, named the most precious, adorable child in the history of the universe, in part after me.

Instinctively, I rub my rear back pocket that contains my father's legacy.

Without thinking, I retrieve Father's badge. Even though I haven't studied it in years, I've carried it all over the world. Through the hundreds of top-secret missions I flew for the Air Force, the birth of my son, thousands of in-service trainings I presented, for decades of time entertaining troops in war zones, and hundreds of calls, I proudly carried my father's badge.

He was fifty-seven. Homeless. All alone, wasting away in a hospital for months before he passed, I think to myself as my vision stays locked on the towering redwood tree landscape.

"And, today, you did it, you survived," I growl in a quiet whisper.

For, like my father before me, I became a firefighter.

I cannot believe that toward the end of my life's journey, I'd have the opportunity to drive mammoth fire engines, be a part of historical wild land fires, be trained on the science of cutting any vehicle known to man to extricate trapped victims, rappel off cliffs, or load dozens upon dozens of folks close to death onto a helicopter. And I certainly never dreamed I would wear a red helmet that identifies me as a captain within my dedicated volunteer fire district of The Sea Ranch on the rugged coast of north Sonoma County. And I never imagined that I'd be able to serve at my beloved Russian River in Monte Rio, which at times is so insanely chaotic that it resembles something straight out of the Wild West.

I proudly gaze at the Monte Rio fire station. "And today, you're here, on your birthday!" I state to myself.

I fully know I should have died several times at the hands of my deranged mother. Toward the end, before my unexpected dramatic rescue, my secret Superman inner-strength core was spent. I just wanted it all to end. Years later as a young adult, Mother unknowingly confessed to me her plans to kill me during the summer of 1973. The "only" problem, she droned, "was where to hide 'It's' body."

I survived all of that in part because of my disgusting past. Besides masking pain and swallowing humiliation, I adapted myself to survive by any means possible. I had to learn to think, execute, and constantly plan ahead while—above all—never lowering my guard.

As a grateful adult, for well over thirty-five years I have proudly dedicated my life's work to try to relieve the pain of others. I so loved making others unexpectedly, over-the-moon happy. But my efforts came at such an enormous cost.

I wasted so much. So much of life's precious time.

I easily gave away too much. I somehow allowed myself to be used and then tossed away. I could have done better. I should have known better. I should have seen things before they exploded in my face, leaving me more psychologically battle damaged and scarred.

To end up alone, only to fume at myself.

And yet, after everything, I'm still here. Amid my imbedded dysfunctions, in my pathetic, pity-party, heart-shattered existence, life moves on. Like billions of others, I'm simply trying to do my part in the middle of a frightening *War of the Worlds*–like pandemic.

Even with all the escalating craziness that I can only imagine becoming worse, I feel God has granted me yet another opportunity. A final blessing. With His will, if I get lucky, clean myself off, step up and out of my pit of despair, I just may have enough summers left to leave a physical legacy for Stephen, his wife, and more importantly, my grandson.

I need to move on. I need to find my place. I just might have enough time to live my remaining days in internal peace. All I need to do is take care of me.

My high-squeal pager suddenly erupts. "Monte Rio Fire . . . 5400 . . . 5435 . . . 5481 . . . Cal-Fire on order, air ambulance notified . . . nonresponsive subject, possible Code Blue at . . ."

Chapter Two
DAMAGED GOODS

IN A SLOW, CRISP VOICE, I deliberately stated to my dispatch center, "Control 2 . . . 5435 . . . clear and available. Thank you."

A flash of a second later, a direct female voice speedily chirped, "5435 . . . Control 2, showing you clear and available."

I quietly released my grip on the microphone rather than let go with my usual quick snap. I then gently replaced the device back in its holder, thus ending my call, making myself and the firefighter teamed with me accessible for any upcoming incidents.

I glanced over at the firefighter sitting next to me. He was so young. He seemed bewildered and overwhelmed. His breathing was still hyper and labored, which showed me he cared. I dared not engage. I felt it best to give him some space in our cramped, rumbling apparatus: Rescue Squad.

After a few seconds, the young man inquired, "Is it always like *that*?"

Because the firefighter was obviously shaken from his first Code Blue, which involved long, intense cardiopulmonary resuscitation (CPR)—that unfortunately resulted in the victim not surviving—I spoke in a soft but reassuring tone. "It's—ah— they're always different. There's a lot of moving pieces on those calls," I stated with a nod.

I could sense from his gaze that he seemed to crave more information. "Okay, here's the thing," I instructed. "By the time we get toned out, minutes have already passed, the R.P.—"

"What's that?" the young man interrupted.

"'Reporting person,' the individual making the call to 911. They've most likely discovered the victim, maybe even tried basic CPR themselves. Then they make the call, explain the incident, confirm the address. . . . We get our pre-tone, jump in the Squad, drive to scene, make room for the ambulance, grab our gear, make entry, move the victim to make space for the paramedics. Then there's barking dogs snapping at us, in these tiny infested condemned cabins, screeching family members, freaking out, blocking your way. . . . Seconds become minutes. It all racks up." The young man nodded. "Seconds count."

"It ain't like the movies," the young man joshed as he turned away to stare outside. After a few beats, he inquired, "So, how many have you—?"

I shook my head.

"Five, ten—twenty—?" he probed.

"Yeah," I caught myself. "Twenty-ish."

"And do you—remem'—?" The young man dug further.

"Yeah!" I snapped. "All of them."

Thankfully the inquisitive firefighter became still for a few moments.

As I continued to drive carefully, part of me processed my experiences—the gurgling sounds, the dark red gelatin oozing from a victim's mouth. Eyes that suddenly snapped open while applying compressions to a victim's chest. And on one call, I was first on scene, literally dragging the person—my neighbor—by his ankles in the middle of the night through a set of narrow hallways to make room for the swarm of rescuers who fought to revive him.

When put together, it all seemed too much.

The firefighter broke in. "And how do you deal with it all?"

"Squire," I exhaled, "truth be told, probably not as well as I probably should have. Everyone's different." I stopped myself before slipping into my darkened past. "Best advice I can give you is don't swallow. Don't bury it. Talk it out. Get it out of your system."

"Okay, man, okay," the young man unconvincingly agreed.

"No!" I strained. "I mean this. You start swallowing, burying things, it becomes habitual, and soon enough, especially in *this* job, it can, it *will* explode into other areas of your life. Without meaning to, it will affect others around you. Others that truly matter, those you truly love. You become closed off. In the end, well—"

My exhausted brain yelled out. *What the . . . ? What are you doing? Get a grip. Back away. Shut the door! Not here, not now!* In my weakened state, for just a flash, I visualized my unexpected loss.

She was beyond gorgeous, with such inner beauty. The energy and sincerity of a glowing child. Long, flowing, well-kept blond hair. Unwavering smile and piercing eyes that could melt the sun . . .

I caught myself. I shook my head as a sign of self-reassurance. "I'm just, ah—saying, in life there are so many potholes, so many dark wells that you can easily fall into. And some holes are hard to crawl out of. And by the time you do, if you do, life, your life, has passed you by. It's gone. *They're* gone. They've moved on." I felt myself tense up. In a near-choking voice I croaked, "You're not even in the rearview mirror."

The young man seemed to understand. He nodded in

agreement as he had hours earlier when telling me about a "he said, she said, she did, he didn't" trivial argument with his girlfriend.

I flashed a smile. "We always seem know that we're angry. But half the time, we forget what *really* made us upset. What exactly *triggered it*. Trust me, it ain't worth the time, your life's time and energy."

I paused, absorbing in part my homespun advice. I then pushed further. "I'm not trying to butt in, but you need to call your lady and work it out, set things right. Don't let it fester. Never go to bed upset. Don't swallow. And, whatever you do, *never* let 'em feel your pain; don't transfer it to those you love."

The man smiled. He seemed genuinely relieved. "You sure know a lot!"

Without hesitation, I chimed, "Young man, what I know is too little, way too late. Besides, any idiot can dole out advice. It's working *through* it that truly matters."

Hours later, in the still blackness of the late evening, I stood outside, sporting a thick jacket and wearing gloves, but I constantly shook from the low-forties temperature. I puffed on my prized cigar. The highlight of *celebrating* my sixtieth. Ever so slowly, I felt my lower back tighten into a taut coil.

It reminded me of the exact pain I had when I was a small child existing in the blackened basement.

I tried to avoid the sensation by deflecting, thinking of something, anything to escape my increasing, wrenching pain. I half hobbled over to the worn bench resting just outside the fire station. I sat on the edge and leaned forward, hoping to loosen the pressure.

I fully knew my physical pain was partly the result of my age, and all the extreme, over-the-top things I've endured. But well before COVID World, it became more triggered from my seesawing, fogged mind. Especially as of late, my past seems to jump into my everyday life just as it had hours ago when dispensing my *ever-so-stellar, worldly,* simpleton's advice. Sometimes, when I've listened to myself as I've lobbed out pearls of wisdom, I railed at myself for not heeding my *own* counsel.

The simple words *Don't swallow* kept rattling inside my head. Out of nowhere, I thought of a person whom I haven't given a mere notion to in years, about whom my beloved foster mother had exclaimed, *"Absolute evil!"*

Mother.

With decades of time and a most unique perspective on life's roller-coaster journey, I don't think she ever had much of a chance. If anybody ingested pain, humiliation, and constant berating, it was Mother.

Even as a preschool child, I understood and saw firsthand Mother's internal battle. At the time, my two brothers and I couldn't help but hear Grandmother's shrilling voice erupt from the phone receiver that Mother would place on the kitchen table. At times, when Father was away at work, even in the late afternoon, Mother was so saddened that she would still be dressed in her worn pink robe, hunched over, clinging to her half-filled glass of straight vodka.

Like a boxer being pummeled by an overwhelming opponent, Mother would take Grandmother's hits. With every insult, Mother's eyes flinched while she rocked her alcohol-swollen face from side to side. Even with her liquid courage, Mother could hardly escape her own mother's spewage.

"You're going to hell in a handbasket. Those children of yours are nothing but hellions; if you don't get control of them now, they're going to rule the roost, just as you and your brother tried to. . . . You'd think with all the hell you've put me through, you'd show a little bit more respect and heed my advice. Since the day you were born, I always knew you'd be nothing but trash, pure trash. Let me tell you something, you think you've got it bad, well, back in my day. . . ."

Nothing seemed to please her. Not even one of Mother's prized Christmas dinners. "Well, if anybody bothered to ask *me*, I say the ham's too dry, the potatoes are lumpy, the gravy's too thick and cold as ice, and most of all, I've seen barn animals with better manners. Children should be seen and not heard."

Years later, on a frigid Saturday morning in the winter of 1973, weeks after my parents separated, Grandmother unexpectedly burst through the front door. From the bottom of the basement, where I sat on top of my hands with my neck strained backward against the head of a nail, I could hear she and Mother tear into each other.

Afterward, both battle damaged, there was a lull for several minutes. Suddenly the upstairs door popped open, and a flash of light flooded the stairs. My eyes couldn't stop blinking from the sudden glare. Standing in front of Grandmother, Mother stated, "Go ahead, look! There 'It' is. Just like I told you. Now, are you satisfied?"

Still winded from her verbal assault, Grandmother huffed, "Well, if that isn't the sorriest child I've ever seen."

In some obsessed primal growl that I'd never heard before, Mother hissed, "And that's the same damn thing you used to say about me!"

Grandmother's venom didn't stop with Mother. She lashed out against Father with every visit. "You should be home more. Why do you have to take on so many extra shifts? You need to stop carousing!"

With a wisp of gray smoke seemingly hovering in front of my cigar, I murmured, "Hurt people, hurt people."

Sitting farther to the back of the bench, I felt my father's thick leather casing that protected his badge. Father, a diehard firefighter who served in one of the busiest fire stations in the nation within the seedy part of San Francisco, for some reason, could not, would not rescue me.

In the beginning, before kindergarten, when Father came home from a twenty-four-hour shift, he would always inquire about my constant state-of-punishment status. And, as always, Mother would fling out some lame excuse. As time dragged on, and as my punishments became more bizarre, Father simply gave up.

Once, when Mother demanded I reingest a hot dog from my school lunch that hours ago she had me throw up, Father watched in frozen dismay. His only form of compassion was a meek promise of "One of these days, I'll have a talk with her. One of these days."

The only incident in which Father almost stood up for me was when Mother crammed a spoonful of ammonia down my throat right in front of him. Seconds later, just as hours ago, my trachea closed. I fell to the spotted kitchen floor next to Father's boots, pounding away in my lame attempt to force my windpipe open. With every blow, I could feel myself slipping way. I gazed up at Dad, still dressed in his work blues, my brave, tall, strong superhero with jet-black hair. He didn't move a single fiber of his being. The best Father could muster was "Hell's bells, just what has the boy done this time?"

With the intensity of an atomic bomb, Mother exploded, "For God's sake, you don't know what It's like. . . . Food, It's always trying to steal food!"

Seconds passed. With every weak strike to the floor, I was close to passing out. I truly felt that I was going to die. From above me, Father then whimpered, "Well, Roerva—maybe—I mean—maybe if you just fed the boy—well—maybe he wouldn't steal so much."

Years later, when my parents officially separated was the saddest day of my young life. Mother dropped off a single box of Father's meager belongings as he stood soaked to the bone in front of a fleabag motel in the middle of a rainstorm. In a rare moment of kindness, Mother allowed him to have a single minute with me. Ordered to stay in the station wagon, I rolled down the window, desperate to grasp Father's fingers. I so wanted to lean my cheek against his skin. He gave me the usual quiet, covert nervous nod. "Just try to be good and stay out of her way. And—ah—one of these days—I'll try to see what I can do."

Without any expression or tears, from the deepest part of my hardened heart, I wailed. I wanted to become invisible and shrink so I could hide in my father's shirt pocket.

One of these days never came.

I removed the badge from my rear pocket, flipped open the worn black leather casing, and rubbed the silver badge, recalling how proud Father was of his career achievement.

In the late 1970s, I was told Father was "asked" to retire early. And since he gave Mother his entire check, at times Father was homeless and survived on the kindness of his firehouse brothers. Other times, he would bus tables and wash dishes at the Tenderloin's Salvation Army, in his words, to "earn a hot lunch." By that time, I was a teenager in foster care.

On rare Sundays, I'd take the rumbling bus from the Bay Area to the end of the line, into the slummiest part of San Francisco. Father rarely met me. Being small and frail and lacking street skills, I was terrified of the army of smelly zombie-like people brushing past me. Eventually I always found Dad in a darkened, dingy bar. With each visit his face became more sunken, and his once-shiny jet-black hair was greasy and clumpy. On one visit, it took me forever to shake Father awake and walk him to the bathroom to relieve himself.

On the bus ride back to my foster home, I thought my chest would explode from my internal heaving. But just as I had countless times before as Mother's prisoner in the basement, I shut it down. It was too much pain to swallow. My mind raced with endless what-ifs: Where would he sleep? What if Father got mugged? Was he freezing on the streets at night? Did he starve? And the terrifying—what if Father died in the middle of the sidewalk and folks simply just stepped over his body—how would I ever find out?

But for myself to survive, I had to flip off the pain switch.

I hated myself for being so selfish. For me it was beyond cruel.

A short time later, on my last visit, as we walked the bustling streets of San Francisco, Father stopped to proudly show me his retired firefighter's badge. In a rare display of emotion, Dad actually smiled, and his skeletonlike, sunken glazed eyes shined. As Father let me hold his leather case that folded open, revealing a shiny badge with an eagle on top, without thinking I blurted, "I'm so proud of you!"

He nodded a thank-you. After Father pocketed his prize, he announced, "I'll burn in hell before that bitch ever gets her hands on this!" I had never heard my father say the B word before. I half laughed, half snorted. I then nodded in return.

Hours later, as he didn't hug, Father shook my hand as I boarded the returning bus. His grip seemed weak, and his skin was leathery. He held on for an extra shake or two. He bent down and coughed. "Live your life. Do what you have to do. Don't end up like me." I lowered my head down at the sorrow behind his meaning. He repeated the last part with an extra squeeze of my hand.

Inside the bus, I stopped at the top of the stairs and turned for a final look. Father proudly stood and patted his back pocket. "Don't turn out like me" were the last words I would hear from Dad.

Sometime later, Father lay in the hospital dying of cancer of the neck and throat. Because Mother refused to let anyone know, for months he languished alone. I was new to the Air Force, nineteen, and naive about matters of death.

When I saw him, Father was barely skin and bones. I could only recognize his eyes. Because of his advanced state, he could not talk, write, or even communicate with his eyes. I stayed with Father for days, enduring Mother's dramatic tirade and justification—"It would be too hard for me to see him"—and a frantic late-night call from Grandmother, complaining about her daughter, my brothers, myself, and the world-at-large.

The next morning I was late. Because of the overwhelming stress and not sleeping for nearly a week, I had overslept. The male nurse told me, "He's waiting to say goodbye." Until that moment, I somehow fantasized Father would pull through. Other people, other fathers died, not mine. This couldn't happen to me.

As I entered the room, the curtains were unexpectedly wide open. The sterile area was flooded with light. With a gurgling sound and strained tiny movement of his head, Father gestured toward the nearby dresser. I obliged, retrieving some papers and his prized badge. I gave him the items. Father opened his badge, patted my hand, giving it to me.

My world stopped. I couldn't believe it.

With time running out, Father and I held hands with the badge between our grasps. Not wanting him to slip away, out of nowhere, I slowly spun the most outrageous lie of lies. As if it were taken from *Of Mice and Men,* I blathered how I purchased a home for us at the river. "It's beautiful. No one would ever bother us or tell us what to do. There will be no yelling, it would be so peaceful. We can sit outside on our balcony. We can watch the sun set. We'll have the fireplace in the winter and barbecues in the summer. I'll take care of you."

Father knew. I'm not sure if he chuckled or tried to smile from my ruse. Then for the first time that I could ever recall, Father kissed me on the lips. Moments later he passed.

I snapped my father's badge casing closed. Dad's death—and, more so, his sad life—had always haunted me. When I turned fifty-seven, the age of father's passing, I was secretly terrified of suddenly dying. It was then that I began to feel myself shutting down—ever so quietly, emotionally pulling away.

I shook my head to clear the cobwebs from my childhood. I forced a half smile as I stared at my beloved towering redwood trees. A thick blanket of gray-white fog covered the trees and the nearby hill. A crisp, unique scent from the trees filled me with peace. Since I was a preschool child, I had been transfixed by the serenity of the Russian River. My most cherished moments, before everything became so insane and when I was still a member of the family, were at the river. The daylong trips to the river, where my brothers and I swam and happily splashed one another or made endless sandcastles and looked up at the ancient dark-green truss bridge. The family hayrides followed by roasting hot dogs on a whittled stick for dinner. The three of us scrambling up a huge, burned-out tree stump, then simply sitting, staring upward at the tallest trees in the world.

My tired mind drifted once again.

I can still feel the sensation of Mommy unexpectedly pulling me into her. Her soft hair tickled my face from the slight breeze. She held me so tightly I could feel her heartbeat. We stayed glued together as loving mother and son for what seemed like an eternity. So as not to break our rare trance, I didn't dare utter a word. We both simply gazed in awe at the blue-and-orange-laced sunset against the background of the trickling sounds from the green river.

That same summer, Father and I shared rare time together.

I rubbed my tired forehead. I fully know I'm damaged. *But who isn't?* I reassured myself. I also realized that I'm not so broken that I can't move on. I just need to get through one day at a time. And with a little luck, I will.

Chapter Three
LUCKY MAN

DURING THE COURSE OF MY LIFE, there have been precise moments in which I felt completely spent and utterly doomed, and yet, out of nowhere, a miracle happened. Looking back at the puzzle pieces, examining different aspects, for me there was no doubt within the depths of my heart that Mother would have killed me. It was inevitable. We were both on a collision course.

On that heartbreaking, cold, rainy day when my parents separated, as Mother drove away, she leaned back and scoffed,

"You're all mine now." With Father gone, there was no way I was going to make it. In the back of the car I quietly recited the Lord's Prayer. When I came to the end, I whispered, "And deliver me from evil. Amen."

Mother had been lobbing her barrage of death threats against me since I was eight. The first time was on a Wednesday afternoon. With no one home, Mother had schemed her elaborate plan to burn me on the gas stove. The next few times Mother made her bold threats, I was just as scared, but my newly acquired super-secret, inner force field kept me from collapsing. Then, over time, I simply paid little attention. To me, it became white noise.

On one Friday afternoon, mere weeks after the separation, as Mother controlled every facet of my life, I blitzed from my school to the house. But this time, for once I wasn't scared. In fact, I was elated. Just a short time earlier my tall, stoic teacher with the Clint Eastwood–like persona, Mr. Ziegler, presented me with a special letter stating I was one of his top students and how on that very afternoon, out of countless submissions, my entry had been chosen for the school's prized newspaper! In my heart I somehow felt this letter would suddenly, magically be vindication for the thousands of times Mother berated me on how worthless and incompetent I was to her and how I somehow always disgraced the family.

As if returning from a hundred-year quest and presenting a long-lost scepter to the queen, I bestowed the sealed letter on

Mother. She quickly tore open the envelope, then scanned the writing. I could tell she was surprised from the way her eyes widened. Mother actually smiled. It was just like the time when I was a preschool child, when she would bend down and spread open her arms so that I could run into her, and she'd give me a deep side-to-side hug.

I had her! I did it! I had indisputable validation that Mother could not hide or dismiss. Out of the countless elaborately planned, painstaking attempts to impress Mother over the last four years, out of nowhere, a simple gesture—"the letter"— would suddenly change my life!

In a voice I had not heard in years, Mother cooed, "Well— aren't you special?"

When Mother bent down, her eyes shined. I so wanted to leap into her arms and press my entire being into her, like years ago while at the Russian River. I had dreamed of this exact moment for years, when Mommy would wake up from our private nightmare and everything would somehow right itself.

Moments later I nearly relieved myself. Mere inches away from my face Mother locked her eyes onto mine and slowly swayed her head like a giant cobra. Then she leaned over and hissed behind my ear, "Get this straight: there is nothing, *nothing,* you can do to impress me. You're nothing. A *nobody.* An *It!* You are beyond disgusting." Mother stopped as if to refill her spent lungs. I could imagine her forklike snake tongue flick my ear. "With every fiber of my being, I pray—for *It*—to die."

In a flash, she tore the letter into pieces. Still in a state of shock, I remained frozen as the precious letter rained down on me like snowflakes.

Hours later, after completing my plethora of chores, I sat on my hands outside on a pile of rocks. I strained to capture any rays of the sun before the late-afternoon fog covered the area. I couldn't help but replay what had happened. I felt Mother's words were no longer from the booze, or from the separation, but from her heart.

And yet, for a mere second or two, I honestly believed my luck had instantly changed. How close I was to a different world. For a fraction of a time, how peaceful and clean I felt. How warm it made me feel.

As low-flying, gigantic shiny planes thrust into the air from the nearby San Francisco International Airport, I felt microscopic. I wished I were a real person. Of all things, I desperately wanted to fly away from danger and take off to somewhere safe.

Even though I felt the end was near, I still foolishly clung to any thread of hope. A short time after my parents separated, Uncle Dan and his wife visited, insisting they'd take the kids to their house for the entire weekend in early March. "*All* of them!" Uncle Dan declared.

Hearing the announcement from the bottom of the stairs, my heart soared! My mind flew into hyperdrive as I fantasized about clean sheets, food that wasn't from the bottom of a sticky garbage can, sunshine, a real bed with a warm blanket, and more warm food.

From above, I could hear Mother trying to wiggle her way out of Uncle Dan's invitation. "Well," she stammered, "I just don't know—we'll just have to see."

Uncle Dan, a hard-core, heavy-drinking, chain-smoking man's-man, didn't budge. "All of them, including David."

I never let on that I had overheard the conversation. I deliberately continued to act meek and disconnected. In submission, I lowered my head into my chest just a tad more whenever Mother berated me, flew through my endless chores a tad faster, and whimpered a bit less when Mother attacked me. She never knew.

Even though I fought hard to bury my weekend escape deep within myself, I gleefully counted the days. I knew Mother couldn't weasel her way out of *this* one.

But that Saturday, when Grandmother made her surprise visit and after the two women screeched at each other, then inspected me like a caged animal, the topic turned to the upcoming weekend.

My ears perked up.

"So," Grandmother began, "I understand your brother Dan is taking the children. Is it next weekend?"

I could hear Mother reluctantly, painfully submit, "Yes, Mother."

Without pause, Grandmother instantly jabbed, "*All* of them?"

"Yes, Mother!"

I almost leaped out of my skin. I nearly allowed myself to squeal with excitement. For a moment, I felt myself floating.

A full second later, I crashed.

In a cold, flat tone Mother huffed, "Come to think of it, The Boy seems to be coming down with a cold. Maybe . . . the flu? I would hate to see the other children get infected. I could *never* forgive myself. It might be best if he stays here, with me."

I could imagine Mother gleefully tapping her fingers together from yet another schemed victory.

Drained from the previous argument and Mother's surprise twist, Grandmother replied, cowed, "Well, a lot can happen in a week."

The moment Grandmother chugged away in her car, Mother summoned me upstairs. With her bony finger, she lifted my chin to her face. Then she hissed, "You thought I didn't know?" She paused for effect. I knew better than to reply. If I did, Mother would instantly smash my face. "I know everything, and I," Mother poked my chest, "I—know—you. Just as you do as I wish, when I wish, how I wish, you hear what *I* want you to hear. *I* know everything!"

To protect myself, I flipped my internal switch and swallowed any emotion that might reveal how crushed I became. While I remained blank on the outside, with every second ticking away in front of Mother, my force-field battery drained like rapid water swirling down a bathtub drain.

From deep within I screamed. I couldn't hold out much longer. I thought my lip began to quiver when Mother announced,

"Next weekend, you're mine. We'll have the entire weekend *all* to ourselves."

Alone in the basement, I kept replaying the words *Entire weekend* all *to ourselves.*

I couldn't sleep. If I nodded off, it was only for a mere fitful minute. As the days passed, I became weaker. In my fog-filled brain, I somehow knew I was reacting exactly as Mother had connived the very day Uncle Dan dared to challenge her.

In my heart, I knew Mother would kill me during the upcoming weekend. I also felt it would not be from some newly, concocted, deviant ploy, but from that extra punch to the kidneys, then when I collapsed, a heavy stomp to my chest, or forcing my head into the soiled toilet bowl just a little longer, or choking me with a more clenched grip for just a few extra seconds.

That Thursday evening, in the bottom part of the house, I covered myself with layers of soiled rags in my attempt to keep myself warm on the decades-old army cot. As I curled myself into a ball, I deliberately did not pray. For years I'd clasped my hands tightly together, uttering my heartfelt requests, "To make Mommy happy, for Mommy to wake up, for me to be a 'good boy,' for me to stay out of *her* way, to be worthy enough to rejoin the family," but the Almighty never heard nor answered any of my pleas.

With a few hours left before my dreaded Friday, I submitted to complete physical and mental exhaustion. As much as I wanted to switch off my connection to God, within the cold silence from the stillness of the house, under the cover of a rag I used to shield my face, I murmured a few words. The very prayer I had prayed on that heart-wrenching Saturday, ending with: "and deliver me from evil. Amen."

Hours later, I was suddenly, dramatically *rescued*.

Through a series of intricate events, I was immediately placed into protective care. By that evening, I curled up in a real bed, with crisp, clean sheets, staring through an open window at a cluster of redwood trees, breathing in fresh clean air.

For the life of me, I never knew why my teachers and school staff suddenly intervened that first Friday in March until I visited Mr. Ziegler nearly twenty years later.

After I worked all day giving presentations at a series of local schools, Mr. Z took me out to an upscale local restaurant. Throughout the day he seemed extremely apprehensive. During dinner we both stumbled to keep the smallest of conversations going. We made little eye contact. As he finished dinner, my teacher cleared his throat.

"There's something I want to get off my chest. I'm not sure if you even know, but—the day when you were taken away, when you came into my class—" My former hard-core, Eastwood-like teacher began to mumble. "You were so small, David, so frail. Anyway, you, ah—you came to class—with no skin on your arms."

I dropped my fork. It clattered on the plate, startling the patrons at the nearby tables. For a moment, the entire room became dead silent. Once again, as it always had in times of extreme stress, my world stopped. I stared down at my right arm. In a trancelike state I uttered, "I remember—gray flakes. Small, dark, grayish flakes. Like patches—on my arms and my fingers." I trailed off almost in a whisper.

Looking pale, as if Mr. Z had seen a ghost, he nodded before confirming, "Yes."

I sputtered out loud. "I was so tired. I wasn't able to sleep. I couldn't stay focused. I always had to think ahead, to survive, to outsmart her. It was all too much. The constant vise-squeezing pressure."

I sucked in more air to my tired lungs. "My God, I can remember everything she did, every word she tried to assassinate me with. But for some reason, I never knew why—"

The fingers to my right hand began to openly twitch, embarrassing me in front of my savior. I plowed on. "It was that Thursday when I came home from school. I wasn't expecting it. Mother did something different. She made her batch of ammonia and Clorox. But this time, rather than throwing me into the bathroom with the mixture, she had me stick my arms into the bucket.

"I somehow felt her wanting to force my head into the bucket. I was so stupid. I remember thinking, *Quick, take a deep breath, close your eyes, keep your mouth shut! You can do this, you've endured worse!*"

I stopped, as if I was self-hypnotized. Moments later, in a low voice, I rambled, "She had me perform my afternoon chores. I was so hungry. I just wanted something to eat. I screwed up. I forgot! I forgot to rinse off the solution." I nodded my head as if visualizing my then-reddened arms through some narrow portal. "That night, my arms were on fire. And the next morning, Friday, because I couldn't sleep, I was so paranoid I was late. I was somehow supposed to get up while everyone upstairs was still asleep, fold my cot in the dark, and begin my basement chores. Again, all in the dark. But I couldn't hold anything, the broom kept slipping from my hands. I couldn't think my way out of it. I thought I was just run-down from all her mind games. Then I remember I couldn't grip the banister to get myself up the basement stairs. I couldn't get the breakfast dishes done—I got so behind—"

Mr. Ziegler seemed frozen at my revelation.

"I was so late. I couldn't complete my assigned chores. Mother had to drop me off at school. When she jerked the station wagon to a stop, Mother instructed, 'Tell them—tell 'em—you ran into a doorknob. Um, tell 'em you got hit with a baseball bat—'"

I paused, surprising myself when I unexpectedly stumbled onto my lost revelation out loud. "Those were her last words to me. I really thought she had it in for me that weekend. And you, you all saved me. You have no idea—"

For a moment, Mr. Z and I joined hands. Neither of us could

control our deep emotions. I couldn't hold back my tears of shame.

Mr. Ziegler swallowed hard. "We all knew, David. For years. Since when you were in kindergarten: the antisocial behavior, keeping to yourself, fits of rage. Then first grade: special speech sessions, fearful of personal contact, lack of motor skills, the way you hunched over, stayed in corners. Snatching food, digging through the garbage. Your attire, how you smelled, the bruises, cuts, the burns—the excuses! We *all knew.*" He confessed, "It was beyond obvious."

"The problem was, back then it was considered discipline, parental rights. We should have done more, sooner. Seeing you when you came into my class that morning is something that haunts me to this very day. We had to do *something.* Our biggest fear was if we didn't intervene, well, you wouldn't make it—"

My savior fell silent before uttering, "I also wanted you to know that you were in our hearts and minds—that, somehow, you weren't completely alone."

I felt the magnitude of Mr. Ziegler's humanity. "I know."

A calmness began to envelope me. "I can never begin to relate what that letter you wrote for me meant. That I was real. That I mattered. Or that Friday when the nurse led me into the teachers' lounge during the lunch break." I gushed, "For me it was like being escorted to the inner sanctum of the Fortress of Solitude. I remember, as soon as I walked in, the room became still. All eyes were on me, including the police officer who sat in the back and gave me a polite nod. I truly thought I was going to jail. And how some of the teachers, who were not used to me, covered their mouths. Some gasped. I felt so humiliated—" I trailed off.

I paused for a beat, then beamed. "Suddenly out of nowhere, Miss Woods, the prettiest teacher ever, came out from the crowd! She strolled over, knelt, and gave me the hug of a lifetime. It was as if we were the only two people in the world. I remember trying to absorb the fragrance of her perfume. When she let go, she stood beside me as some of the teachers came over to say goodbye. I remember you were the last person before the police officer whisked me away. You said, 'You're a *good* boy. So, please be good.'"

"I—I, ah—don't remember." Mr. Z nearly choked.

Without thinking I blurted, "I do! I remember my second-grade teacher, Miss Moss, who confronted my mother after she burned my arm. She mailed me a postcard of Mount Kilauea when she vacationed in Hawaii! The school nurse, who fed me pieces of French bread and, on Fridays, rewarded me with a Twinkie. The kindness of my social worker, my loving foster parents, and so, so many folks along the way. Every random act of kindness fell into my lap at the precise times when I needed validation the most.

"When you're nothing, when you feel less than zero, those small gestures, simple inspirational words, become your universe. Your deed, *that* letter, gave me something to draw from when things became too dark and I nearly got swallowed up. It made me want to be a good person, a better person. A real person!"

"David," Mr. Ziegler stated, "Maybe we all got lucky that Friday. But you, young man, made your own luck!"

Somehow, I managed.

ଔ

There were countless instances when I was at the end of my rope, and yet somehow, seemingly at the last moment, things came together.

I quickly learned while in foster care that when someone told me, "No, it's never going to happen," or "Not a chance in hell!" it somehow made me want it more. I fully knew it was, in part, a coping mechanism from my time with Mother, but I made it work for me.

Years later, when I initially tried to enlist in the Air Force, the two recruiters openly scoffed at me. I fully understood. The last thing they desired was a high school dropout, a former foster child with horribly low test scores. What they didn't see was my inner tenacity.

When not working at any of my scores of menial jobs, I spent my free time—such as it was—at the cramped recruiting office, reading every brochure and even proudly shining their shoes from my worn wooden shoeshine box.

One afternoon I caught a lucky break when one of the sergeants asked his partner, "Hey, what's 1263 divided by 3?"

Before the recruiter could reach over and seize his hefty "pocket calculator" from his desk, from below, as I buffed the recruiter's shoes, I whispered, "Four twenty-one."

A few seconds later, the man blinked in surprise. "So, what else do you know?" I stood up and pointed at the various pictures of airplanes, rattling off the type, manufacture, and what theater certain planes flew in combat.

When I saw an older black-and-white picture, I pointed, "Chuck Yeager. Retired one-star general. World War II fighter ace. Flew P-51 Mustang named after his wife, shot down, escaped, and evaded and flew again. First person to break the sound barrier with the Bell X-1, August 1947—" I paused and smiled at the recruiter's stunned face.

Out of nowhere, it was the unexpected break I needed. After that one incident, both men took me more seriously. They began to understand my internal dedication.

So, as always, I "ground it out." I showed up at the office four to five times a week. I retook a battery of tests to up my scores. Next, I obtained my GED. Then I filled out mounds of paperwork detailing my time in foster care and my placement in so many homes, all the while carefully skirting around that I was abused.

The hardest challenge of hiding my past was not from the various psychiatrists but the medical doctors. One in particular had me repeatedly explain my slumped shoulders, my burned tongue from swallowing ammonia, and my lack of simple dexterity. I nearly lost it in front of him on one visit as the doctor grilled me relentlessly about the scar on my upper chest. "And this one?" The doctor poked with seemingly morbid pleasure.

Standing in front of a stranger with my pasty, skinny frame wearing a pair of worn briefs, shaking, I coldly replied, "Accident."

"Accident?" the man repeated as he flipped through paper after paper. "I'm not buying this. It doesn't make any sense. You do realize, if you lie, if you're not forthcoming with the truth to any question, that will mean grounds for instant dismissal. Period. And from what I understand, you're no prize as it is."

I felt insignificant, exactly as I had when Mother would berate me for hours on end in the dead of the night. I almost told off the doctor. Yet before I could erupt and spew my lava of buried shame, the doctor shook his head in dismay. "I just don't get it."

I surprised myself by how quickly I felt so intensely enraged. I had always admired and felt safe with doctors, especially after my first moments of being in protective custody when I was taken to the hospital and how everyone was so gentle and took tender care of me. But this man, how I wanted him to feel my pain.

It was the same flashing sensation I had wanted to release when I was humiliated and beaten constantly by the schoolyard bullies when I was in foster care. I was attacked and pummeled almost daily in junior high. The list of reasons was endless: I was always the new kid; I didn't fit in; I was too geeky, too weird, too awkward, or too small; I dressed in worn, cheap clothes. The saddest one was from an oversized boy named Tony: "My mom's boyfriend beats her, so I beat you."

I had convinced myself, once I made my way into the adult world and far away from towering imbeciles and teenage thugs, my buried issues would never arise. Then I could start my life clean.

One time I lost control. Ron was a tall bully in high school. When our fight was over, I stood over Ron, who was lying on the hallway floor in the fetal position with his huge, bloodied hands covering his face. When I limped away from the scene, the hushed group of gawkers quietly stepped aside.

Even though I felt a sensation of revenge and even righteousness, part of me hated myself for how I acted. Even when Ron was down, shielding his face, in my rage I still hammered away.

That wasn't me. Of all things, I didn't want to journey down that dark path like Mother.

I was most fortunate to not lose it in front of the doctor. I was too close to that edge. Had his inquisition lasted a few seconds longer, I might have spewed my feelings all over him and thus finished any chances I might have made for myself with the armed forces.

In all, it took nearly six months, but after I filled all the basic requirements, the recruiter called me in for the official interview. "Here's the deal," the recruiter hesitated. "I like you. You're a scrapper. But because of your scores and—well—your background, all I can offer you is what we call 'Open General.' It means, if you enlist, you could be assigned to drive a garbage truck or a bus, or be a field cook God knows where." The sergeant paused as if to let what he stated settle. "It's bottom rung on the ladder. But at least you can enlist."

"How long would I have to be bottom rung?" I dared to ask, knowing that a door to a real opportunity for a better life had finally cracked open.

"Three, maybe four years, a full enlistment, until you can possibly, maybe, apply to cross-train for another job? And if you do, your scores have to improve dramatically, and I highly recommend you take some specialty courses before applying. You're going to have to make an extreme impression."

"Three, four years?"

"Again, no guarantees," the recruiter warned.

I reconnected with that quiet surge of pride. *You've been through so much worse,* I thought.

As a young boy, after Mother accidentally stabbed me in the chest, to escape my dread, in my fantasy world, I became Superman. On the outside, I *appeared* to be weak, of little value, and didn't fit in. But deep within, where no one could see, I was invincible. I could overcome anything!

So, I affirmed to myself, *you drive a bus, sling some hash. Big deal. After all you've been through? You've got this! You can pull through. You can do this. One more time!*

I stared past the recruiter. My eyes widened. Behind him, the calendar date read mid-August. I had officially aged out of foster care over six months earlier. My caring foster parents had allowed me to stay on until I got myself together, yet they stressed I had until the end of the summer to move out.

Once again, my life's timing was in sync.

"One other thing," the man said, "I am in no way obligated to tell you this, but in some cases we do a bit of a background check. I spoke to a couple of your teachers, a Mrs. Woodworth and Steven 'Zigalar'—"

I felt myself shrink.

"Just hear me out." The sergeant tried to calm me down. "Some kids come in here and blow past everything—test scores, aptitude test, physicals—everything's easy-breezy. Everything just drops in their laps. No sweat involved. There's no sense of pride, no ownership. Not a thread of strain. They get a little cocky. Half of them crash in basic training, first time they've had to find a way to work things out. But you," he shook his head in admiration, "you just didn't cave in."

I shook my head, returning the gesture, signaling, "Thank you."

The recruiter stood up. "I'm talking about *then* and *now*." He paused for a long moment as if he was trying to make a deep inner connection. The sergeant maintained eye contact just as my broken father had before I boarded the bus, when I received his final words of advice. The sergeant continued, "This opportunity can change your entire life. *You* can really make a difference. I want you to make the most of this. It's gonna be a pain, but again you're a scrapper." He extended his hand. "I expect good things. And I truly wish you Godspeed, Airman Pelzer. Welcome to the Air Force family."

I shook the kind man's hand. "I'm all in!" I beamed with pride.

That singular opportunity, at that precise time, changed the course of my life.

A mere five years later, the impossible became reality. I pinned on my prestigious air-crew wings. As always, the task was years long. It felt insurmountable. And I received a rare opportunity because I was days away from outprocessing from the Air Force due to endless debacles in misplaced paperwork.

Then, just a few years later, through a string of events, while still in the service and working part-time in juvenile hall, I did public speaking about resilience. That led to providing rare in-service training throughout the state, then nationally, when I hung up my flight suit and was honorably discharged from my Air Force family. That years-long string of events led me to eventually publish a book that was dedicated to my teachers.

I've always contemplated my luck.

CR

Days after my sixtieth birthday, I lumbered up the Northern California coast to my home in the remote community of The Sea Ranch. I slowly, deliberately drove at a snail's pace, staring at the charred steep hills from the explosive fires of the previous year. At one hairpin curve, I recalled driving a fire utility truck after dropping off much-needed equipment for a Strike Team crew, and how the Ford was pelleted with baseball-sized rocks from the battering winds and fires just hours earlier. My only concern had been the possibility of explaining to my beloved chief, Bonnie Plakos, how I somehow wrecked two apparatuses in a period of a single month. I subconsciously rubbed my still-sore neck, the result of my unexpected crash to avoid a head-on collision by mere inches as a speeding car veered in my lane.

I exhaled, recalling some of the events as a firefighter in the last few years: the fires, a major flood, working in sleet mixed with rain during the middle of the night, cutting trees, cutting cars, rappelling off cliffs, and loading countless folks in helicopters, hoping, praying for their best.

And the deaths. Three boys in a speeding car. Children unable to escape from a burning home. The thundering, crashing sounds of fire—debris whizzing by at two in the morning as thousands fled from walls of flames from the infamous Tubbs Fire. Yet the worst sensation was hearing and feeling the distinctive thud from frames of houses collapsing after a massive fire engulfed hundreds of homes in a matter of minutes.

So many devastating events, brought upon so many unfortunate folks, filled me with dread.

⊗

I back my SUV onto my gravel driveway. Before I open the glass door to the beautiful unique glass and concrete home, I sigh another quick prayer, thanking God for my safe return. I open the door and step into a long, narrow hallway that is barely a few degrees above freezing. I pass a room filled with packed boxes. I shake my head in sorrow.

I'm moving. Only a handful of people know.

Partly, I'm way too ashamed to announce my departure.

In a matter of weeks, the new owners will move into this spectacular upgraded home that sits behind a nearby teal-blue ocean bluff.

I've clung on for way too long. As much as I am devoted to my firefighter family, I have to move on.

It is literally for my own good.

For decades, I've devoted myself to God, country, and parts of the world and everyone I've ever come in contact with. My sole purpose was always to try to make other lives better, brighter, and more vital—happier. And now, unexpectedly alone again, I must do what's right for me, what makes me feel safe.

I'm fully aware that I have very few summers left. I'm also fully aware of my health and my increasing physical limitations. God, life's mileage, and the extreme nature of my past as well as overzealously serving two intense fire districts have educated and humbled me all too well.

I am now way too exposed.

A lifetime ago, in my early twenties, when I had thick, blond hair and a slim, taut body, I once blitzed a six-minute mile. *Once!* Pushing myself further, I also sprinted ten to fifteen miles at a time in boots. Decades later, I arrogantly wore heavy fire-utility boots sixteen-plus hours a day, seven days a week, for almost ten years. Now, with thinning salt-and-pepper hair and a noticeable midsection, my feet have become so beaten, I cannot walk five feet to the bathroom without excruciating, shocklike pain.

Yet the biggest secret I've hidden from everyone was my scarred trachea. Nearly two decades ago, after a battery of tests, I was diagnosed with a herniated esophagus and trachea, in large part from ingesting Mother's ammonia. I was instructed to lay off spicy foods, wine, and cigars, and refrain from public speaking. That all lasted a full twenty-four hours. I couldn't resist my very own prepared spaghetti sauce, with extra spices!

❧

A short time ago, while on a fire, I slipped. While laden in full turnout gear and mask, I could feel my trachea suddenly closing. Automatically, I've trained myself to relax, not panic, and stretch my neck backward while reducing my breathing. But the stress of my fire detail left me spent. I nearly threw up in my mask, and a fellow firefighter had to help me up. It was then I realized I was not only putting myself but others at risk.

After years of hiding, masking, and lying to myself, something *has* to change.

I must change.

I must move forward. I have to move.

I have no place to move into. In part because of the lack of housing exacerbated by the local fires and folks fleeing the concrete jungle of the Bay Area with wads of cash, there is literally nothing available. I have started to have recurring nightmares as I did when my father was homeless. Yet I've already purchased furniture, electronics, office equipment, and a cadre of military deployment–like items ranging from pots and pans, towels, and rugs to even an Asian water feature. I want everything to be new, fresh, and clean.

In my multilayered, hyperintense mind, I can see it all come together.

The countdown has begun. I am beyond terrified. I can't sleep, I eat like a bird, I can't keep any food down, and I'm overly exposed.

With all the pain, the devastating loss of hundreds of thousands in America alone from COVID, and hundreds of millions affected by the worldwide pandemic, I feel selfish pleading for the grace of God to bless me with that rescue luck one last time.

Chapter Four
THE ODYSSEY OF SLEEP

ALONE, IN THE DEAD OF A COLD WINTER'S EVENING when my world is still, I think. I dissect events, down to the smallest detail. I draw out situations or contemplate life-altering nano-moments. *I should have said this. I could have done that.* Or hours later, as my decades-long insomnia takes full reign, my brain splinters off with endless *Back to the Future* space-time-continuum scenarios. At times, I convince myself that during the course of my life, I could have reached out, opened up, or spoken up—not shut down or erected a hardened wall around my heart. It might have made all the difference.

Everything in my world would be *all* so different. Maybe, my mind spins, I wouldn't have lost the ever-so-gentle "Mrs. Atomic Blond," "*The Princess Bride*": the lovely Kay.

When I plummet into *that* state, I know it's time to crawl back into bed for a nap before officially starting my day.

But I rarely sleep. Then, when I do, it's seldom restful.

My mind hardly ever completely spools down. There always seems to be something: some unforeseen monumental crisis that I must solve for others, some project, some event to prep for, or some *thing* I *may* have said or *may possibly have done,* in a heartfelt, best-of-intentions error, that I need to—that I must somehow—vindicate. It's always *something.*

Therefore, I rarely let down my guard. To do *that,* I have to feel safe.

It's a sensation I've had before, in my days of shivering, with layered sets of wet, smelly rags I would use as a blanket of sorts on the World War II army cot in the basement.

I first noticed my issue when I was around four. After an all-day visit with our grandmother in San Francisco, Mother drove us home. My two brothers immediately passed out to the point that, when arriving home, Mother forcefully shook the boys awake. But I noticed, on the trip home, even though I closed my eyes, I could not relax until I was wrapped in my very own cocoon blanket in bed. And even then, I had to quietly rock myself to sleep.

As a scared preschool child, I had already adapted to heighten my defenses. During my time in the basement, I quickly learned to always keep my radar on, no matter how utterly physically or psychologically exhausted I became.

If I dared to shut down, if I got caught, the consequences would be dire. And yet, at times, whenever I rarely, stupidly took the chance, it always seemed to backfire with a vengeance. One mistake, among others, still affects me to this day.

ଓଃ

It was a cold early evening in winter.

Upstairs, the family was stuffing themselves in the dining room with one of Mother's elaborate dinner meals. Spirits seemed high. I imagined clattering plates of bright steaming food being passed back and forth.

In a different world below, I caught the sounds of laughter bursting from one of my brothers.

Usually I sat at the bottom of the stairs. At times, I'd cheat and remove my hands out from under my buttocks while resting my strained neck. I would steal a few minutes of precious sleep.

Yet, for some time, Mother had me stand in a corner behind the mail slot. I was never completely sure why she had moved me. Once I overheard my brothers complain that they were tired of having to look at me whenever they ran up and down the stairs. Or it was simply just another of Mother's deviant schemes that it would be more grueling for me to stand perfectly upright, with my hands glued to the sides of my legs. The most depressing part was watching the misty cold air seep through the rectangular mail slot seconds before it penetrated parts of my bare skin.

Since I was constantly exhausted from the new position, I quickly adapted. I found I could cheat by leaning my upper body against a thick wooden stud. I would close my eyes for a good ten to fifteen minutes of pure, much-needed rest.

My challenge was that the more I stole tiny moments for myself, the more I desperately craved them. I began to rely on my escapes too much. They became addictive. At times I foolishly allowed myself to shut down.

But I always listened to every creak from upstairs. I analyzed the pattern. When there were no longer any sounds of scraping the dinner plates or when the family chatter subsided, I would soon be summoned. I especially became aware of the distinctive sounds whenever the upstairs door flew open, followed by the booming echo of Mother's heavy feet as she marched down the stairs.

One time I had stupidly lowered my guard. In my stupor, I could sense everyone was still eating. But out of nowhere, I heard the deafening, rumbling sound of Mother turning on the water for the upstairs bath. I felt safe as I knew if she came downstairs to get clothes for her boys, since it was dark, she'd have to turn on the light. I wanted to cling to my escape world just a tad longer. I calculated I had a six-second window for me to easily snap back into position.

Mother would never know.

In my sleep, I sensed a sudden coldness. It was as if I had stepped into a deep freezer. As uncomfortable as it was, I didn't want to let go. Ever so slowly I opened my eyes. I tried to focus on the slot of the mailbox, thinking a gust of fog had pushed through. Seeing nothing, I became scared. From within, as if I had jammed my finger into an electrical socket, I jolted myself fully awake. *Wake up. Focus. Think, now!* I commanded myself. The lights to the basement were still off, the raging sounds of the upstairs bath continued, and I didn't hear the slightest stir. *Okay, you're safe,* I reassured myself.

But I sensed something was still way off.

When I was initially banished to the basement, I truly believed that huge hidden snakes or alligators were inches away and would suddenly gobble me alive. Being a small child, I'd clamp my eyes shut, praying for the sensation to pass.

Standing by the mailbox, my eyes strained to open wide. My racing heart made me feel light-headed. I fought to control my breathing as I carefully turned to the left. A few seconds later, I was relieved because nothing was behind me.

I gave thought to returning to my private sanctuary. But as I turned back to the right, the figure of Mother stepped forward and came into full view. As if pleased with herself, she revealed a disgusting smirk. Mother's sudden appearance terrified me with such force, I half jumped backward, striking the back of my head against the wooden stud.

I never allowed myself to fully lower my guard in Mother's house again. I conjured up different ways to try to steal rest while somehow keeping my internal radar turned on. Over time, my yearning to shut down overwhelmed my linear logic for my safety.

Yet through a near-death experience, I completely submitted. Through that, I unexpectedly became empowered.

03

I was ten. It was the middle of summer, days away from the Fourth of July. By then I was worn down from lack of food, nonexistent sleep, and the constant tension of how to outthink Mother. With no school, it meant no food for me to steal, so I was always beyond hungry. By then, I was only able to rest in short, few-minute bursts while never forgetting the mistake of my past. As much as I craved food, I longed more for the escape of sleep.

After the family finished their dinner, as always, I was summoned upstairs, then, as commanded, stood like a statue while Mother ranted at me on the conditions under which she *might, possibly, maybe* feed me if I completed my duties in hypersonic time.

In part because of not being fed for days, coupled with my

lack of sleep, my mind was in a state of fog. My eyes were heavy. I closed them for a fraction of a second. I think I fell asleep right in front of her. "Look at me when I'm talking to you!" Mother roared.

As I fought to refocus, Mother seized a knife from the nearby counter. "And if you don't finish the dishes on time, in twenty minutes, not a single second more, I'm—I am going to kill you!"

Her words had no effect on me. Even my baby brother Russell, who strolled over and began rocking on Mother's leg, wasn't fazed by her incensed threat. This was all so normal within the household.

Then for dramatic flair, Mother waved the knife. As she had done this before, her flurry had little meaning. My sole concern was for Mother to simply shut up so I could finish my chores on time and might have the chance of something to eat.

But something was off. She seemed more than her inebriated self. Her voice seemed overly loud, the gestures, all more dramatic. *And yet still—?* I cautioned myself.

Feeling I could collapse at any second, I strained to focus, to pick up on a mere thread of a clue. *Focus,* I calmly informed myself. *You can do this.* Relaxing my strained eyes I saw it. The combination of her half-glazed eyes, the thrusting, waving motion of her right arm, as Russell amplified his rocking on Mother's clamped leg. She looked like she would teeter over at any second. I almost smiled. For a second, I gave in to the thought the Satanic battle-axe would fall flat on her face.

Then I saw it.

I should have ducked, sidestepped, yelled, anything, done *something*, but like a frightened animal trapped in truck-sized headlights, I froze. I couldn't believe it. *Mother of God*, my brain announced.

It was a slight blur. An unexpected gasp from her mouth. Mother's sudden eye-popping horror on her twisted face.

Before I felt it, I wanted to stop our world. I wanted to flee to "Mommy," embrace her, and with all the love of the universe, and ever so gently, whisper beside her ear, "I know. I know—you didn't mean to do this. I know, it's an accident. *This* is an accident."

In my reality life, a full second later, my chest exploded. In my shocked state, I strained to clearly see the tip of the carving knife covered with blood. I wanted to lift my head, to lock on and offer a smile to Mommy. My legs seemed to splinter. My eyes closed. I free-fell into a gooey, dark abyss.

I regained consciousness only for a few moments before I fell back into my hole. In those rare flashes, Russell danced above me chanting, "David's gonna die. The boy's going to die." In other streaks, I focused on Mother's busy hands trying to apply pressure to my seeping wound. She struggled to wrap my ripped T-shirt around my gash. I wasn't scared. Before marrying Father, Mother studied to be a nurse. Whenever a neighborhood kid scraped an arm, Mother was calmly in charge to save the day.

In one longer flicker, we both locked eyes. We held our gaze for a second or two. Like a household pet dog whose master had mistakenly stepped on his tail, I so craved for Mother to know that I forgave her, that *this* wasn't one of her premeditated, vengeful attacks.

Watching Mother's frantic hands, *this* was serious, something she could definitely not conceal. From deep within, I was relieved. I simply waited for Mother to scoop me into her strong, protective arms and race me to the hospital. In my fantasy mind, I saw myself cleaned up. Wearing fresh, clean clothes. Resting in crisp, white sheets, in a warm, sun-filled room.

It was not meant to be. After bandaging me up, Mother announced I now had "thirty minutes to do the dishes!"

I was beyond shocked. I couldn't believe it. Her words seemed to echo as if driving through an endless, narrow tunnel. No hospital. No apology. No hug. Not a simple gesture of basic kindness. Mother treated stray dogs with more compassion than she did me. And just as Mother had years before when she accidentally pulled my arm out of its socket, and years later when Mother informed a nosy teacher about the blister-ridden burn on my arm, she fully intended to keep the accident a private family matter.

With Mother's clock running, I had no time or energy to feel sorry for myself. Just as I had vowed to myself years before—after Mother burned my arm—that I'd never cave in,

I would finish the stupid dishes. I'd show her! Even if it took me the entire night, I'd complete my task. I'd give it my all, I'd give it my best!

That evening, after changing more T-shirts from my seeping wound, then allowing me to eat a few scraps of food, Mother stood vigil over me as I tried to sleep on the green army cot in the basement. Surprisingly, she even soothed, "It's going to be fine, you're going to be all right," while she bent over and dabbed my sweaty forehead with a cold, wet cloth. In some strange sense, I desperately wanted her affection.

I almost felt safe enough to escape into my dream world. But when I entered it, I found myself covered in sheets of red hot rain. No mattered where I tried to flee, the rain followed. I could not escape. The next morning, my chest and face were crusted in dried rust-colored blood. Mother came to greet me by flinging a rag at me, informing me to clean myself and begin my chores. "You're already behind."

Unfortunately, three days later, and with Father away at work, things were back to normal. I sat at the base of the stairs shivering, but not from the cold. Because Mother insisted my wound wasn't all that bad, she demanded I continue to perform my household chores. My injury did not have a chance to heal. If anything, the slit seemed to expand. It became dark, with mustard-colored and white ooze seeping out. My face became drenched with sweat from my increasing fever.

I was trapped. I knew if I dared to walk up the stairs and ask

Mother for medical care, she'd thrash me without thinking. With my luck, she'd probably pummel me directly where I was stabbed.

I had to do something. I seethed at myself for my current state. I still realized that if I went to Mother, I'd lose. If I continued to sit, I'd lose. *Do something?* I gently asked myself.

"That's it!" I announced to myself. "Just do, *you* do, something!"

The answer was right in front of me. The cleaning rags.

I felt like a burglar while sneaking over to the basement sink. I was taking an extreme risk. If Mother opened the door and didn't find me at the base of the stairs, she'd beat me senseless.

But my fear of possibly dying overrode Mother's potential reprisal. After wetting the tip of a rag, I carefully pinched the slit. A split second later, it was as if I were shocked by some electrical current. I nearly knocked myself out by striking my head against the gray concrete floor.

I so wanted to cry, to purge my deepened pain. But at that moment, I didn't pine for my lost mommy, nor did I desire possible help from my passive, reluctant, "one of these days, I'll see what I can do" father. I just desired to do something for me.

I was beyond scared. I felt locked, trapped in my own web of shame. In the darkened, cold basement, tears uncontrollably ran down my face. I felt like a pitiful little crybaby. I hated myself for always being so scared. Always being so sad, so pathetic, such a weakling.

With trembling hands, I wiped away my tears and studied the slash. The thick yellowish goo began to ooze. I knew that was a good sign. "Come on," I challenged myself. "Do this!"

With every second that slipped by with me doing nothing, the chance of my exposure increased. I felt for sure Mother would check on me at any moment. Before I could chicken out, I grabbed another rag, stuffed it in my mouth, then pinched behind the slit, over and over and over again. With every squeeze, I screamed into the rag. Even though I felt I might faint at any second, I continued to pinch until I saw blood.

Sensing my time was close to running out, I half limped, half crawled back to the base of the stairs. Even though my raggedy shirt was soaked with my tears and yellow ooze, I was relieved to see the droplets of red. I somehow felt the wound would heal.

I was proud.

It was at that moment I sensed it: that warm, inner-confidence sensation. I was *not* as weak or sorrowful as I had outwardly projected. On the inside, where no one could ever begin to imagine, I was indeed strong. For years upon years, I had endured and overcome so many of Mother's freakish games. *And you're still here,* I cheered to myself. The spot of blood was my latest victory, perhaps my biggest triumph against her humiliating, crushing pain.

I could feel myself drift away. My head no longer rang like a church bell. It seemed so light, as if I were floating. In a baritone voice, my brain played, *Mild-mannered basement boy able to overcome, outthink scheming evildoers, seemingly from another planet. Look up in the sky! Up, up—and away!*

At the bottom of the stairs, out of pure exhaustion, I submitted. I took a daring chance. I completely shut down. I fell into a deep relaxing sleep. I dreamed.

I was flying. Flying away from danger. Flying toward somewhere safe. I wore a bright red cape. . . . I was Superman.

∝

Some fifty years later, in the middle of another chilling night, I stand alone outside listening to the thunderous, crashing echoes from the nearby waves. In part because of my loss, I crave restful sleep like a hopeless addict.

My childhood insomnia has crippled me far beyond my days of being with Mother.

The very first night as a foster child, I dreamed that Mother was chasing me while wielding a knife. I somehow felt her snarling breath just behind my neck. In the next six years of foster care, my nightmare still had Mother gripping a massive, gleaming knife, but with me trying to flee through an endless dark maze. The only way I was able to escape was by waking up, heaving and drenched in sweat.

My initial days in Air Force boot camp, I stayed awake the entire time at night, waiting for some unexpected thing to spring up. Later as a swamp cook, I only rested after my weekly shift, going without sleep for days at a time. When I became an air-crew member, I never slept the night before my thousands of flights. Just as I had applied my time in the basement, conjuring up outlandish ideas to steal food, as a young crew member I applied my time studying every sequence of every page of my checklist. Then I'd imagine various in-flight emergencies and how I'd instantly thwart them. At times when I'd deploy overseas, while other crews rotated to rest, I'd stay awake and hyperalert for the twelve-plus-hour flights.

Years later, as a civilian, when I crisscrossed the world, some-times traveling more than two hundred days a year, I'd take a few-second nap during the plane's takeoff roll, but after liftoff, I'd be wide-awake for the rest of the flight.

Yet for some ominous reason, I rested well while serving weeks at Hurricane Katrina; at Joplin, Missouri, after the tor-nados; and even in the midst of Middle East war zones.

Back home, it doesn't help that the pager I constantly wear squawks several times a minute. At times, it seems that when-ever I limp home from my lengthy shift from Monte Rio, after opening the house and putting things in order, as soon as I lie down, my pager erupts with a notification: a call. I am in no way obligated to respond to every incident, but at times it takes me out of my multiyear pity party.

The mature, rational reality is that with the intensifying

suffering of COVID World, I have no justification to become overwhelmed by my loss. I'm fully aware of my endless blessings, and in my role as a first responder, firsthand, I see good people on their worst day.

Yet with passing months, I feel myself slipping away. There are times when I have the same sensation as I did before my rescue, my lack of rest giving in to foggy thoughts. At times I truly believe I cannot endure my deepest pain. There are moments when I have dark thoughts.

I try to put things in perspective. For me, on a bad day, after returning to my seaside home after a fatal call, I immediately strip off every article of clothing, throw everything in the wash, step into a nearly scalding shower, and scrub myself. Afterward, I cover myself with thick body lotion, then dress in a fresh set of duty clothes in case I respond to another incident. I then stand outside with a cup of coffee, or if I decide not to respond, something much stronger.

Searching for peace, as always, I quietly pray.

Back in time, on my critical calls, I came home to Kay.

Late in the evening, after getting clean, I'd carefully slip into bed and spoon tightly against her. I'd pull Kay into me enough to feel her soft exhale. With my right arm I extended it so that my fingers could wrap around my bride's flowing hair. I'd give her strands a gentle tug just to hear Kay's unexpected murmur. At times I would drift off as we breathed in the same rhythm.

Since we first became lovers, I always felt safe enough to fall deep asleep with her.

With Kay, I could submit.

❧

A chilling gust shakes me from long-ago intimate memories. I gaze upward at the endless sea of silver stars against the bright moon. I wonder if my former beloved is awake. With her passion for astrology, maybe she's gazing up at *da Luna* as well.

Before we moved to The Sea Ranch, I had promised my bride an upscale telescope. Kay could have easily reached out and pocketed the stars. *Her* stars. Yet between the military-like deployment of moving to The Sea Ranch; decades of unexpected, grossly mismanaged tumbling finances; and a laundry list of everyday, time-consuming events, I failed to fulfill my simple promised gift.

The winds pick up strength. I hear a faint internal mantra that has permeated my psyche for the last few years. You promised. *You promised you'd always take care of me. . . . You promised.*

I had fought too long, covertly holding everything together. I stretched myself way beyond various cliffs.

Our union slipped through our fingers.

I blame myself.

I should have done more, been there more for Kay—physically

and in every other supportive way. Yet with all my grandeur and over-the-top efforts, I failed.

With my mind becoming numb, I offer another quick prayer before returning inside where I encase myself through a series of heavy, precise sliding-glass doors. After another bad day, I am physically clean and layer myself with fresh PJs.

I flop onto a soft, cloudlike mattress, with thick clean sheets. And just as I had when I shivered on the dank army cot, I wrap myself into a cocoon. I roll over to Kay's side of the bed. I spoon a long, narrow pillow, pulling it tightly against my upper body. Then, out of reflex, I extend my right arm while rubbing my fingers until I give in and drift away.

Chapter Five
THE LONG SUFFERING

I STAND ALONE OUTSIDE the Monte Rio fire station, absorbing a rare moment all to myself. The seasonal weather is beginning to warm, allowing my stiffened lower back to relax just a tad. My body is constantly tired. I'm exhausted in more ways than I can count. Between driving up and down the coast to serve two separate fire districts, packing, assisting with the recent rollout of COVID vaccinations, and meticulously making my former Sea Ranch home more beautiful for the new owners, plus various Zoom meetings, I have no time to recharge.

My once-instantaneous *Beautiful Mind*—with its problem-solving and connect-the-dots abilities—is close to being fried from the increasing pressures from every direction and from multiple levels. My life seems consumed with pushing through one problem, only to have three or more needless, numbing situations spring up and take root like wild weeds.

On top of everything, I sense something else. A subtle, creeping sensation of building tension. It seems constant, from everyone, from everywhere. Folks snapping at one another at the grocery store while trying to hoard mountains of toilet paper. Full-on arguments while filling up at the gas station, and especially the increasing frustration of waiting in line, much longer than before, at the beleaguered post office. It all seems inescapable. At times, it seems like being inside a pressure cooker.

Months ago, I noticed an exodus of sorts. A true-life *Grapes of Wrath.* Couples of all kinds and herds of families escaping the concrete jungle of the Bay Area, fleeing to the remoteness of The Sea Ranch. At Monte Rio, just across from the fire station, at a parking lot used as a homeless encampment, I have a clear view when fights suddenly erupt, with three or more brawls per day. At times, they go on for hours and late into the evening. The police are so overwhelmed and scattered that unless one of us firefighters sees a knife or any other fatal object, there's little for us to do. Depending upon the known characters, at times

I'll notify my partner and retrieve the medical bag, knowing we'll soon have a walk-in.

The late-night brawls, drug overdoses, and suicide attempts that were sporadic events have now become the daily norm. The influx of more folks brings more DUIs, which creates more traffic collisions and more dangerous vehicle extrications. In one month alone, the station ran over 110 calls. As compared to the North Sonoma Coast Fire District at The Sea Ranch that tallies around 200-plus calls annually, Monte Rio has officially become the *Wild, Wild West*.

Yet what pains my heart is seeing the endless rows of cars, campers, and RVs strung out on various Monte Rio side streets. While some are in fair condition, the majority are beyond dilapidated. Then, once parked, the vehicles can leave only when towed away after they've been abandoned. I once counted twelve people living in a midsize camper. During its heyday in the Big Band era, Monte Rio was advertised as "Vacation Wonderland." But now it is engulfed with the homeless strain. A few miles inland, upscale cities on the street to my gym have been dubbed "RV Alley." At times, the milelong street becomes so choked on both sides, it makes it almost impossible to thread one's car through. When I saw a small Hispanic boy—five, maybe six years old, with thick, matted black hair—crawl out from a tent set up on the roof of a car, I lost it. It somehow triggered the last few years of my father's pitiful life.

It all seems like a slow, anaconda-like squeeze. I've seen the stress creep up and get the better of a few young, brand-new

Monte Rio firefighters. One unleashed his obvious displeasure during the middle of a medical call in front of a shocked patient.

On the slow drive back to the station, the young man vented, "Gawd, I'm sooo sick of this whole sheet-ball show. You can't pay *me* enough for this. Why do I bother showing up? I don't need this. I hate it here. It's beyond disgusting. Every day, more calls, more piss, more vomit, more shit. God, they smell! How can they stand living like they do? Do you know that some of them actually live under the bridges?" He seemingly informed more than asked. "And did you know we had a fire under the one by the station, last summer—?"

I turned my head, giving the young man a quick, hard, nuclear stare. For a moment I felt like the main character from the movie *Gran Torino*.

The young man seemingly had a shovel and wanted to put it to good use. "You should have been there, man. You could have seen me. Total, bitchin' sheet-show. Thought we had some loser trapped behind a shield. I kicked major ass on that one. That's what I do. Jump in, kick ass, 'n' take names. I'm the real deal. Hard-core, *all the way*. That's me!"

Liar! my brain fired off.

I know because that was my call. I was the only firefighter on that shift. I ran the station, Han Solo, by myself that Sunday. My boss, Chief Baxman, and I were first on scene. In weighted gear, I clumsily struggled to get over a fence with thick, overgrown vegetation while pulling a charged reel line with one hand and carrying a wild land tool in the other. Once under the bridge, I had to shoot water through a small opening, pushing the smoke and fire to the other side. Then on my knees, I frantically dug under a thick, long, rectangular piece of metal being used as a lean-to. My serious quandary was that with every scoop of dirt I freed, I'd lose my purchase. I fully knew I was putting myself at risk. I probably should have radioed that I was coming out. I was extremely close to sliding down the steep concrete incline that made a vertical drop into a rocky dry creek.

But I picked up a distinct smell coming from the other side of the shield. In a flash of a second, it reminded me of my worst call: two girls trapped inside a fully involved structure fire. In the dark of night, even with a dedicated team of over twenty firefighters at the scene who were there for several hours, we couldn't get to the precious babes.

Sucking in a quick breath, I tried to free a corner of the thick shield. By pulling it down and to the right, I pulled myself with the metal. I could feel myself about to tumble. My only thought was to fling my tool down and away before I fell onto it, possibly stabbing myself. Out of pure luck, someone grabbed my waist from behind. It was my old friend and one of my initial instructors from Cal Fire, Captain Pat, with a crew of three eager young firefighters. "Thank God," I breathed.

Afterward, back on flat ground, I was debriefed. The fire was started by an individual who tapped his extension cord into a nearby streetlamp. From the other side of where I made entry, there was a tiny camouflaged crawl space. Inside were a flat-screen TV, two PlayStation controllers, an air mattress with an electric blanket, and a hot plate that was cooking a steak. The squatter had strolled over to the nearby store to pick up his daily six-pack when the fire broke out.

It took another two hours to put the "Type 6" Wild Land apparatus back in service, including replacing a 150-foot hose. Because of the dark of night, with no light I had stupidly pulled the wrong lever, thus accidentally charging the line. Once water is introduced into the hose, it must be drained, then stretched out to dry afterward. I was most fortunate to have a local volunteer assist me.

Mr. All the Way, Real Deal was most likely tucked away in his childhood bed, as he still resided with his mother. To the dismay of myself and other firefighters, All the Way once had the gall to openly complain about his mother—who cleaned his room, washed and folded his laundry, changed his sheets, and even packed him a bag lunch—infringing on his privacy whenever he wished to hook up with a young lady and sneak her into his mother's house.

I silently drove the Rescue Squad back to the main station. I took a deep breath. And as I was taught in my tai chi classes, to maintain more critical oxygen in one's body when stressed, I extended the tip of my tongue to the roof of my mouth.

Of all things, I didn't wish to seethe. I could never reveal the deepest, tar-filled, black-pit trigger of my hidden inner self.

And yet I fully knew Hard Core was nothing but a sadistic bully, that he thrived on needlessly pummeling and belittling others to feel ultra-superior. My movie trivia mind instantly expelled a line from an Indiana Jones film: "Nazis. Jeez, I *hate* those guys."

But like my days in the basement, as always, I swallowed. I kept the obvious to myself.

My saving grace was that I knew, the chief knew, and Real Deal had to know he was a wannabe, a blowhard. I've seen his kind more than a thousand times—those who have never been pained. Never, if needed, crawl on glass with a broken ankle, or sprint with all their might with no oxygen in their lungs for the sole purpose of maybe, possibly being of service to others. It was the overt arrogance that stung me. Even sadder was whenever All the Way acted all toughy-tough in front of the much younger, more impressionable firefighters; they bought into that persona, allowing All the Way to venture further in his web of deceit and toxic behavior.

I so wanted to state the obvious. To *finally* put someone like him in *his place*. I could feel myself ratcheting up, just as I first had when I survived in the basement.

ॐ

Back in the day, on a rare Indian-summer afternoon at the beginning of the school year, the neighborhood hosted an im-promptu block-party barbecue. It seemed as though everyone on the street had their grills blasting away. The distinctive smell of charcoal filled the air. Every child seemed to explode with bursts of laugher as they whizzed up and down the block on their bikes. Sitting on my hands on the concrete floor facing the corner with my back to the open garage door, I could make out the unique sounds of baseball cards that were clipped on the bicycle wheel spokes.

Behind me there was a flurry of activity. My two brothers, Ron and Stan, flew up and down the stairs retrieving food, condiments of every sort, and endless bottles of soda. Ron was especially proud because Father was allowing him to cook for the very first time. With all the nonstop hustle, I couldn't sneak a nap or remove my numbed hands, and I had to keep my neck strained backward, as commanded, in case Mother walked by. All I could do was close my eyes and wish myself away.

I might have dozed off. When I opened my eyes, Ron was standing nearly beside me. I turned my tightened neck to the right. Above me, I could see droplets of sweat on his face. I assumed it was from cooking as well as from bouncing up and down the stairs. For a moment I thought it was odd that Ron didn't take an extra step so I could see him better and help relieve my neck.

"Man," Ron let out a long exhale as if he had just run in the Olympics, "you should see it. It's crazy. So much food. Burgers, dogs, chips, beans with bacon. Brownies, cakes, pies. Just crazy. Everybody brought everything. There's no way we're gonna eat it all. No way. That's going to be such a waste."

With the last few words, Ron changed his tone. It dropped an octave. He slightly shook his head. It reminded me of—it took me a few seconds to figure out: "Oh—my—Gawd," my brain analyzed. "Mother! He's speaking just like her. In that cold, disconnected, cruel, deliberate, sarcastic manner." I turned my neck farther to look into my brother's eyes. He had a weird smirk. He seemed to have a gleam of twisted pleasure behind his eyes.

I couldn't believe it. Not Ron. Out of anyone on the planet, not him.

When we were small children, because Ron was the oldest, before Father went off to work, he always instructed the elder son, "When I'm gone, you're the man of the house. Look after your two brothers." As Father finished his instructions, he always seemed to nod at me.

I had always felt Ron took his assignment to heart. When I was first banished to the basement and whenever Mother allowed Ron and Stan to make a sandwich snack, Ron always flung me a folded piece of bread with a layer of thick mayonnaise. Later, as we bumped into each other, my savior would covertly whisper, "Air mail surprise!"

The mayo surprise seemed like a lifetime ago. Looking past Ron's black eyes, I calculated why he didn't stand in front of me. First off, he had to know I was in pain sitting on my hands. Second, by not standing directly in front of me, I'd have to impair my stiffened neck all the more. But last, the cruelest, just a few inches from my cheek, was a freshly grilled hamburger, with double patties, oozing with thick orange cheese. I smelled the greasy beef before my eyes could fully take it all in. It was so close, if I were an alligator, I could have easily leaped up and snapped up the entire prize.

Whether he intended to or not, Ron squeezed the buns. A small stream of mustard and mayonnaise splattered on the floor. He saw me looking at the condiments. Another smirk escaped his mouth. Then another strained exhale. "Such a waste, man." He shook his head before turning away. "Total waste."

I felt my own brother, like Mother, was baiting me. I couldn't resist. All I had to do was lean to the left, slowly slide out my right hand, and quickly finger-scoop the warm, grease-drenched condiments. *Slow down,* I informed myself. I took a deep breath and began to lean leftward—but stopped before scooting my hand out. The most important thing I had to do was listen. Before exposing myself, I had to feel safe and ensure that no one was about to stroll through the wide-open garage door.

I gave it a few seconds. I felt sure of myself. But I heard something that made my ears perk up further. Without thought, I rocked my body back to right. At first, I thought I was hallucinating. I knew I was tired, but not to such a level that I was hearing things that weren't real.

My chest began to race. I fought to quickly slow it down so that I could hear better. It was subdued, but somehow clear, as if just outside the garage. "What did she 'fling out' this time?" A lady asked.

Another woman coughed before answering. "Sick. He's still sick, very sick. Doesn't want to expose him to the other children. Says she'd never forgive herself if the others got sick."

"He must be the sickest child on the planet. If you ask me, that's just a load of manure," the first lady proclaimed.

The second voice chimed in. "Mark my words, one of these days she'll go too far—"

A new voice spoke out. "Do any of you even know the boy's name?"

The second voice immediately replied, "Daniel!"

Inside the garage, I winced. *I'm so invisible. I don't even exist.* Part of me wanted to appear outside and announce my existence.

Outside, the first lady adamantly spoke up. "David, the child's name is David. My Lord. And have any of you ever noticed, she never says his name? Ever? Calls him 'the boy.'"

A fourth woman spoke up. "The only time you see that child is when he runs back and forth from school."

"I see David," a thick, hurt-filled voice broke in. My next-door neighbor, Alice, stated, "From my bay window. I see that poor child sitting on a pile of rocks, with practically not a shred of clothing on, shivering to death."

I heard a quick series of short gasps.

They care, I told myself. I was real. I mattered. *They* knew. Mother's death-grip secret was becoming known.

The first lady announced, "Someone should say something."

Another voice echoed, "Someone should *do* something."

And another voice, "What can we do?"

The second lady: "Who do we call, the police, social services? I just don't know, but for the love of God something has to be done."

Another series of murmurs, as if nodding in agreement.

Some lady coughed while another lady overly loudly cleared her throat. From inside the garage, none of the sounds rang true. A happy voice broke out. "My, oh my, Cathy Pelzer, if this isn't the best salad ever, I surely don't know what is. I must get that recipe. You look so pretty in that dress, how do you do it all?" I heard the other hens cluck in agreement.

I slumped my head forward. For an unexplained reason I felt so close to escape, perhaps closer than ever before. Mother couldn't stop all of them. It was beyond obvious. Without a shred of doubt, I fully knew I could run faster than my brothers if they gave chase.

My mind tapped into my most private of secret protective cloaks: *Faster than a speeding bullet. Able to defeat evildoers at any cost, willing to crawl on glass, more powerful than mere lazy mortals.*

I veered back to my other fantasy. "The ladies," I told myself, "they'd protect me. They'd shield me!" I felt a surge of elation.

I closed my eyes. "No, you can't do that. You can only rely on yourself. Don't be stupid! It's simple, so simple. Just run! The door's open. Just weave through all the people and split. This is it; you can do it. Run, David, run!"

With my eyes still closed, I saw myself suddenly springing up from the concrete floor. Then I'd walk perfectly erect, as if I were a hardened cowboy with no name who just rode into town, stepping into a rough bar. I'd show no fear. I wouldn't hesitate to stare at all their shocked faces. I'd stop for a moment to take in their gasps, as I breathed in the scent of burned charcoal and hamburger grease. I'd growl in a deep voice. I'd state the obvious: "The name's Pelzer…, *David* Pelzer. I'm no longer your slave. I'm no one's slave, not anymore. I'm real. I matter." Then, at the precise moment, just like a gunslinger about to pull out his set of pistols, I'd snatch as many burgers as I could before blitzing away at breakneck speed.

I opened my eyes, exhaling. I was near tears, but I couldn't open that lockbox. I knew I could never stand up for myself. I would never do anything like that. I *couldn't* do anything close to that. All I could do, as I'd always been trained to do, was swallow. Swallow any form of worth. Ingest my gulf of shame and the constant, deep, degrading well of humiliation.

I glanced over at the stained floor. Without analyzing, calculating every mere series of micro-moves, I tilted to the left, scooted my hand out from under me, and scooped up the multicolored condiments from the dust-layered floor before sucking my sticky finger clean.

I was almost proud. At the very least, I did *something*.

I wasn't overly depressed about my episode for lacking guts and not sticking up for myself in front of Ron—or for not being my own person and simply ending what everybody knew about my state by announcing my presence and simply walking away.

The sticky mustard/mayo remnants on the lifeless, filthy floor were more than I'd had before. At that moment it was good enough for me.

∞

Inside the cab of the Rescue Squad, the radio crackled. "5435 . . . , Control 2, status check."

"You did clear us from scene, right?" I asked All the Way, who shrugged his shoulders and gave me one of his distinctive "sheet happens" looks. Seconds ticked away and still no answer. While my job as the driver was to safely get us to and from a call, my partner was responsible for navigation and radio transmissions. "Ah—you going to respond?" I asked while pointing at the microphone. I widened my eyes, signaling, "Hey, man, the dispatcher's waiting."

My partner grimaced, "Chill out, ol' dude. I've got this!" Without looking, as if to show off, in a flash All the Way snatched the wrong microphone and shouted into dead air. Then he seemed stymied. Staring at the radio, he gave it a grimaced look when dispatch did not acknowledge his transmission.

I quietly exhaled. In a deliberate, calm manner, I grasped the correct device and stated in a low, Steve McQueen–like voice, "Control 2, 5435, Code 4. Show us Clear and Available. Thank you."

Old man, thinning hair, no country! I told myself.

Before I could release the spring that allowed me to speak into the microphone, Hard Core lobbed, "Ain't no big *thing*. You gotta learn to *chill*; otherwise we might be using dat AED [automated external defibrillator] on you pretty soon, Pops!"

I knew the last word was a deliberate jab. I also knew that once we returned to the station, our boss, Chief Baxman—at times an overbearing persona and a stickler for the minute details—would eat his lunch for not clearing us, forgetting to grab a medical bag and the AED, and not having on gloves and mask before making patient contact: the basics.

Every firefighter makes mistakes, every day. Myself more than anyone. I made more mistakes in part because I did more than the average firefighter. I put myself out there. While some stood around chewing the fat, I engaged more. I did lots of small things, big things, everything. I didn't overly mind messing up in front of others, but I made damn sure I didn't repeat needless mistakes. And most importantly, I owned up to my blunders. To me, Hard Core lacked the most important element a person of service should have above all: a sense of humanity.

"Hey Old Man," he asked. "Your sweatshirt, says 'Ain't no S.A.C.' What's dat mean?"

How appropriate, I thought to myself. I gave the young man an off smile. "'Ain't no Stand-Around Clown.'"

He shook his head. "I don't get it." He seemed lost in deep thought. After a few seconds All the Way stated, "'Clown,' I get it. You sure are funny, for an ol' dude."

That was the third jab in the last few minutes. I knew the kid was trying to get the best of me. It's just how he was, and how a fair amount of his generation acted.

However, looking at it in a different light, the young man was right. To him I must be a fossil. And I felt it. I've been feeling it creep up on me for years. When I first became a volunteer firefighter, I took every specialty class I found and every physical test my body could stand. I trained five, sometimes six days a week at the intense Cal Fire level. Whenever I failed a "training evolution," which was quite often, I repeated it over and over and yet over again until I felt I had a basic understanding and felt safe.

The hardest evolution for me was simulating first on scene, Han Solo, for a structure fire. I had to give a report on conditions, park the engine in a certain fashion, and engage the water pump. Once out of the cab, wearing heavy turnout gear, I'd chock the wheels, then deploy the 150-foot attack line, flaking it out in a certain manner. Next, I'd throw and extend a twenty-four-foot ladder, placing it precisely next to a second-story window. I'd then return to the engine, grab an axe, and carefully open the correct valve that charged the hose. Next, I would put on my self-contained breathing apparatus (SCBA). Then I'd take off my glasses, go on air, and make my way up the ladder, with the axe on one side of my body while holding on to the nozzle with my free, gloved hand. Finally, I would use my legs to lock in the rungs of the ladder and deploy water.

It's a timed evolution, with many parts that one can fail if certain aspects are not accomplished correctly. The Cal Fire pros make it look so effortless. One young engineer, Ryan Felix, my instructor for the event, knocked it out in nine minutes! After three full-on attempts, my best time was thirteen minutes. After my first try, I was completely spent, but I had to try to push through. On my final attempt the entire crew of five firefighters half cheered and half jeered me on as I clumsily struggled up the ladder.

As physically challenging as that particular evolution is, for me it's just as mental. One has to pay attention and break things down that can save time *and* one's energy while being safe. While some firefighters put on their SCBA first, I'd put it on last before I scurried up the ladder, which saved some energy from the unnecessary weight. And I always ensured my legs were locked in the ladder as I slowly cracked opened the nozzle that releases a minimum pressure of 125 pounds. One fairly new firefighter made the error of popping the nozzle open like a pressurized cork from a Champagne bottle. Since one of his legs was not fully locked onto the ladder, with that suddenly intense pressure, he nearly flew sideways off the tall ladder.

After I stripped off my gear and downed several bottles of Gatorade, Ryan hovered over me. "You certainly ain't no S.A.C."

Sitting down, with sweat literally pouring off of me as if I had just stepped out of a shower, I chimed, "It's not so much the age, but the mileage."

Less than a decade later, I know there is no way I can come close to my best time for that exercise. With every year I can feel myself getting slower, weaker. I saw it when I worked out. Years ago, at my peak, I (stupidly) curled forty-five pounds per arm. At age sixty, I can barely curl thirty pounds. I once bench-pressed well over 200 pounds, now I can hardly lift 135.

For me the real eye-opener was the firefighter pack test. It's a forty-five-minute drill as part of the list of requirements to be qualified for Wild Land Fire Strike Team deployments. For the pack test, one wears 45 pounds and has to walk on a flat surface for a distance of 3 miles. Because there are no level areas at The Sea Ranch, it makes the test a bit more laborious, as there's one steep incline. In addition, one has to complete two laps around the small airstrip next to the fire station, which totals 3.3 miles. The first time I put on the 50-pound lead vest, I could barely breathe. Weighing just over 180 pounds and looking at the road wet from the early morning rain, I thought I was about to bite off more than I could chew.

I felt I had to try, just as I had calculated every step as a child when I ran from school, during lunch break, up the hill to the local store. I stole any item of food my desperate fingers could seize. Then I blitzed back down, returning to school a mere minute before the bell signaled the end of break. After the unfamiliar first lap around the airstrip, like my time in the basement, I broke down segments and calculated where I had to be at certain parts for my second lap. It paid off. I completed the test in just under forty-one minutes.

Wanting to build up more stamina and confidence, I made the pack test part of my workout regimen four times a week. At times, to shock my body, I'd put on my laden Wild Land web gear that carried three gallons of water and other tools, including a Pulaski tool and my radio, adding an extra thirty pounds. After one lap, I'd slowly walk west, away from the fire station and down a steep grade to the coastal Highway 1, then back upward and without stopping to the Cal Fire complex.

I was quietly proud. The more I trained, failed, and still pushed through, the more the Cal Fire personnel treated me as one of their own. In a short time, I became a court jester of sorts, with my zany, off-the-cuff movie lines and impersonations.

Unfortunately, time, age, and events slowed me down. Just last spring, maybe in part because of COVID restrictions and not being able to work out as much as I needed, my time on the pack test was a disgraceful forty-four minutes and twenty-four seconds. Even though I passed and still covered an extra third of a mile, I felt completely ashamed of myself to have slid so far in the short amount of a year's time.

As I was huffing my way back to the Cal Fire station, for some reason the vest seemed so much heavier than before. I poked at one of the newer seasonal firefighters, "Hey, are you guys messing with me? Did someone add some weight to this?"

The young and polite firefighter, whom I'd given the handle of "KGB," seemed taken aback. "No, Cap. If anything they had me take out five pounds the other day, to make it more legit."

"Five pounds?" I shook my head at myself, then apologized to the young lad. All I could think about was the movie line, "Man's gots to know his limitations." I thought about my foot injury while hiking up and down hills in full Wild Land gear while laying out over a thousand feet of hose with my partner, in the dead of night, during the dangerous Tubbs Fire of 2017.

I had a fleeting thought. I immediately flushed it away. I loved my firefighter family.

ભ

Hard Core broke my reminiscing. "You know, I've been thinkin'. I'm not so sure 'bout this firefighting gig. It doesn't pay enough for all the hours. I know I can do better. If it doesn't work out for *me,* I know for a fact the military will want me. Special Forces, Airborne. All the way, that's me, baby. They'd probably give me one of them signing bonuses. Hell, I could be one of them drill instructors, kick ass, take names, let everyone know who's the boss. Hell," he gave me a jab on my upper arm, "if you don't croak, I might just come back an' teach an old dog like you a new trick."

Damn it! I shouted at myself. This arrogant dolt will—not—let up!

I could feel my insides tense up. My head began to ring. Part of me wanted to explode onto him. Mr. Kick Ass was way too much to endure, for way too long.

◌৪

It was the exact sensation I had felt when I was in the fifth grade, after being continually taunted by my classmates on one Friday afternoon in the winter of 1973.

I was already stressed out and exhausted. I zoned out during Mr. Ziegler's lesson. My eyes were glued to the thin black hand of the electric clock as it dragged its way to the end of the school week. In a short time, I would be in Mother's House of Hell. I used to pray for time to freeze. I used to fantasize that, with my superpowers, I could somehow stop time. And that I'd stay in the warm classroom, and then at night I could read books of high adventure before I'd curl up to sleep under one of the tables in the school's library.

As I had since the first grade, I absorbed the kids' jabs. It was all so normal. In a way, I felt, I deserved them. I did smell. I stole their food. I was always hunched over. I stuttered like an idiot. *So, yes,* I convinced myself, *I was a spaz.*

But the tone from Clifford, the schoolyard bully; another classmate who never failed to inform me to "drop dead" on a daily basis; and her overly macho friend John—that afternoon the three of them seemed colder, crueler than ever.

In part because of the building of my stress-filled exhaustion, I let them get under my skin.

As I kept staring at the clock, three spitballs struck the side of my face. It seemed as if the entire class quietly snickered with their hands over their mouths. Without thinking, as I should have done that afternoon at the barbecue, I sprang up. I stared down at the set of bullies who sat clustered together. I opened my mouth.

I wanted to proclaim, "God, I wish I were *you*! You have anything and everything. You have food, clothes, a home, a bed with clean sheets. You think you're all so tough? Do any of you think you could survive one second of a single day like me? Do you? You've never been beaten till you pass out. You don't have to dig through garbage for a scrap of food like some rat. Ever swallowed ammonia? Been thrown in a room with ammonia and Clorox? Have any of you been choked so hard that you can feel your eyes burn?

"Damn you all to hell. Do you think I like any of this? That this is how I wish to live?

"I'd give anything be you! You're no one's slave. You're not invisible. You matter!"

That's what I wanted to scream, what I had practiced in my

head hundreds of times. Another part of my fantasy was for my surge of hatred to somehow hit them all row by row as if I had the power of a hydrogen bomb. For once, I'd make others feel the pain that they'd all dished out to me!

That's what I wanted to do—what I so wanted to say—but in my pathetic reality, all I could muster was bowing my head in submission, before stuttering some obscenity before I fled the room. My only outlet was slamming the door with such force I truly thought the rectangular panes above it would shatter. Then, like a little preschool child, I fled to the bathroom, hid in a stall, clenched both my fists, and pounded at the floor as I cried.

❦

"Hey!" Blow Hard chimed. "Did I tell you I kill it on *Call of Duty*? And something else, I saw that movie *Gettin' Private Ryan*—"

I let out a slow breath. "'*Saving*.' It's *Saving Private Ryan*," I corrected, as that movie was one of the most compelling films on the horrors of war and also the dedication of humanity to a worthy cause.

"Yeah, whatever, Pops. So here's the thing. Had I been there, they wouldn't touch *me*! I would have taken out all dem Nazis. I would have sooo—"

Inside my tired brain, I finished, *Kicked ass!*

As my partner for the day continued to blather away impressing himself, with the station in sight I made a right-hand turn onto Moscow Road. I slowed the Rescue Squad and began counting the train of RVs and campers. I prayed not to see that young boy from the tent.

"Whatcha' doing?" Kick Ass inquired.

Part of me almost slipped. I wanted to state, "Our job." Instead, I calmly said, "There's at least seven more RVs than last week."

"So?" He seemed confused.

"So, this whole COVID thing is getting worse. Even with the vaccines beginning to roll out, it's not going to solve everything overnight. It's going to take years, and even then, it's never going to be the same. Folks can only take so much. So many are strained past their limit. So many have since lost their jobs, their entire livelihood, their self-worth, everything. Before *this,* a lot were barely hanging on. For some," I pointed at the vehicles, "this is their last stop."

For once Blabbermouth listened. Borrowing his line, I continued. "Here's the *thing.* In this job we see some great folks on their worst day. And at the river, we see the worst of folks on their rock-bottom day.

"It's about being of service. Something bigger, better than yourself. It's never about kicking ass. It's about extending a hand. Sometimes a word, a gesture, a random act of kindness can—"

Kick Ass let out a sneezed laugh. I knew I lost him. "You sound like one of those old geezers from some history class.

Man, you need to chill with that. This is the twentieth century, you're too old school."

And you're obtuse! I fired off to myself, knowing society was well into the twenty-first century. I almost chided him by asking, "Hey, did your parents have any kids that lived?"

After turning around, I drove by the infamous parking lot that I had dubbed "The Walking Dead," as it was filled with homeless folks who at their best had a tent. They filled their day by milling around at a snail's pace. I made it a point to study my partner's face, searching for any reaction. It only took a full second for him to telegraph his response.

All the Way let out a huff. "If you ask me, they're all losers. Every single one of them: losers!"

I gently brought the apparatus to a stop and made sure I placed the shift handle in the park position. This was a long, painful time in coming. "Just who do you think *you* are?" I calmly grilled. By the sudden contorted look, Bad Ass seemed taken back. Before he could fire off some random, elementary school playground retort, I dug in. "Do you—have you ever given a thought, a single idea, to how these people got here?" I deliberately paused. I wanted the question to truly sink in. "Have you ever given an iota about *their* plight? Do you think they woke up one day, sat around the table, and proclaimed, 'I'm gonna be a doctor.' 'I'm going to be an astronaut.' 'I'm gonna be a teacher.' Hey, I wanna be *homeless!*'" I paused a beat. I wanted him to *feel* it, just as I had with my then classmates, or those folks at the barbecue as they gorged themselves, and every time I swallowed others' indignities!

Feeling myself about to spool up, I stopped. That wasn't me. He was just some punk-ass boy-child who would probably not amount to too much. I knew if I did, it would only make things worse. Besides, I informed myself, I was better than that. With age and life's experience, I knew better.

I switched tactics. "Last month, we had that call: fall victim, head injury. Remember?" I flung out.

"Yeah, I hate blood. Grosses me out. I totally thought that ol' geezer was going to bleed out," Kick Ass replied. "So what?"

"You never asked, 'What made him fall?' Treating the injury is literally a Band-Aid. It's like when I worked with folks new to a 'program,' drugs and alcohol anonymous. To just stop using or stop drinking is not enough. It's *what put them on that path* that led to their demise. A lot of these folks," I pointed at the parking lot, "never had a chance. No parents who cared for them; some ran away to get away from abuse, rape, being treated like garbage, you name it. Some fell on hard times; some still haven't recovered from the crash of 2008. Some literally lost their homes to the fires. In the last four years, in *this* area alone, we've had the Tubbs Fires, one massive flood, two mandated evacuations from still more fires, and now *this* armageddon, *War of the Worlds* virus. . . . Some made mistakes, stupid frickin' life-altering blunders. Who hasn't?

"I'm the most blessed person I know, and I sooo have screwed up more than anybody. I've been lucky. But for some, they never caught a single break. They kept hitting every branch on the jinxed tree of life. Some fell into holes that they could never crawl out of." I had to pause to catch myself.

Bad Ass sneered. "Yeah, what do you know? You've got it made. You've got a nice ride, you live up in Sea Ranch, you're rolling in it. I bet you've never had a bad day in your life."

I remained perfectly still, not stating my obvious. I wasn't a bit offended. I did, however, instinctively rub my finger, still feeling my ghost wedding band.

I put the shift handle back to drive. As I made my way back to the station, I calmly inserted, "My father was a firefighter, San Francisco. One of the busiest stations in the country—*hard-core.* The *real deal.* Truly a *bad ass.* Served for decades. My parents, they separated. Never divorced. He gave my psycho mother every cent. I mean every cent of his paycheck. Ended up sleeping in alleyways, cardboard boxes. People used to step over him as if he were garbage—one of San Francisco's finest. Fought in World War II, had a wife, eventually five kids." I stopped, staring into my partner's eyes. "Such a waste," I lectured, thinking of my father's plight.

I continued, "He got meager pay. But for him it was never about da money. Even when he was homeless, my dad still served. He'd do odd jobs, anything he could scrounge, sweep floors, wash dishes, just to earn a hot lunch. One time, when I was in foster care, my father took me to the Salvation Army in the grungiest part of the city. He was so proud. They treated us like kings. Best roast beef I ever had."

Hard Core seemed transfixed. "Wait. Hold up. You was in foster care. No way! What for? That must have sooo sucked for you. I mean, you seem to have it together—for an—"

I quickly cut him off. "What you don't know about life, real life, can fill the Grand Canyon. Everybody makes mistakes; some folks are luckier than others. It's just some mistakes, you never can pay for." Again, I rubbed my finger for the phantom ring.

I stopped and concentrated on backing up the Rescue Squad to just outside the station's bay. I kept the engine running after placing the shifter into park. "I may be old and gettin' slow, but I'm wise enough to know I am the luckiest son of a bitch the world's ever seen. But I've worked hard for my luck. I know what it's like to be less than zero, which is why, like my father before me, I choose to serve." I stopped to inhale a breath of fresh air.

"This COVID thing is going to tear a lot of folks up, rip a lot of families apart. So *here's the thing*: you can choose to step up and to be part of the solution, and be of service, or shut up and step aside."

"Holy sheet-balls!" Hard Core shouted. For a second I thought he was reacting to my heartfelt speech until I turned to the left. Just in front of me, an elderly homeless man was dragging himself from the parking lot as if he were a *Night of the Living Dead* zombie. He waved an arm that spurted blood.

I could clearly see that his lifeless hand was bent backward. By the look of his pasty white face, I thought the man could faint at any second.

Bad Ass seemed frozen. His eyes were fixated on the homeless person. "Ga—gross—"

"Hey," I snapped, "Grab the med bag. Have him sit down. Keep his arm above his head. Don't forget your mask and gloves. I'll be right behind you."

I snatched the microphone. "Control 2, 5435. Walk-in medical. 9870 Main Street. Adult male, hemorrhaging below the wrist. Possible broken hand. Request tone out, request medical."

Before I finished, my free hand was on the lever to the door. As I opened it, my partner remained frozen in the cab. "Hey, Hard Core! You coming?" All he could do was give me a vacant look. He gagged as if he might throw up. Outside the cab, I grabbed the heavy medical bag and turned on my mobile digital radio. As I put on a pair of purple latex medical gloves, I growled to myself, "*Call of Duty,* my ass!"

Chapter Six
NOW BEGIN

I'M LOSING IT.

I feel as if my inner confidence has somehow slipped from my grasp.

I realize my emotions are a potpourri of adapting to the increasing stress of COVID World, being a first responder, moving, struggling to find a place to live, a heart-wrenching divorce, leaving my firefighting family, and dissecting my life. Yet, I *know*, I *feel*, I am a shell of the person I used to be. From deep within, I have no battery stores to draw from. I feel I've foolishly exposed my life to too much kryptonite.

On the outside I still act affable and comical, but at a single layer beneath my worn shell, as of late, I truly detest myself. I can barely look at myself when I shave. With all my journeys, meeting millions of folks and studying hundreds of biographies on exceptional and even notorious individuals, while others have endured nothing but despair, I've never known anyone who has received God's favor and protection more than myself.

I feel I've wasted so much.

I've become haunted by the decades upon decades of the complete waste of atomic power–like energy I've spent on relationships or crusades that, in the end, amounted to absolutely nothing. I'm incensed with the blessings I've been given—that I could have, *should* have, applied myself in other areas that would have truly made a difference.

It always happens in the early morning hours when I can't sleep. Especially when I return to the safety of my lifeless Sea Ranch home after a critical call, I process—overprocess—anything. Everything.

When my cluttered mind spools down and begins to relax, some answers from decades-old questions from life-altering, fork-in-the-road situations filter through. I discover things that I didn't see then or wasn't safe enough to open myself up to and examine during the course of my *then* life: things like speaking up, raising my hand to question the obvious, or not swallowing so much unnecessary crud. Maybe I should have pushed harder or backed off further or even sooner. Or been less judgmental against others who I felt wronged me and in doing so hurt me much more than I ever revealed.

Standing outside, I gaze at the microdot sheets of fog that push in from the nearby cove. I stare upward at the field of pulsing, silver-white stars. In rare instances when the moon radiates an orange-brown glow, I raise my hand as if I can cradle the satellite in my outstretched right palm.

Back in the day, whenever I felt depleted, I'd look at my right arm, take in a deep breath, and become recharged. I'd suck it up. I'd do the unthinkable. I made things work out. At the very least, I'd dig, and dig in more, if need be, and try to attempt and do *something*.

In the still of the night, I gaze at the back side of my arm before extending my fingers. I study the length of my forearm. I then rotate my wrist back and forth while stretching the palm of my hand farther.

A sincere, rare, slight smile escapes me.

I recall the very day when Mother held my arm over the lit gas stove for several seconds. After letting go, I crumbled to the floor. Above me, Mother ordered me to strip, then lie on the gas stove and "burn for her." With Father at work and my two brothers away at their Boy Scout meetings, I felt trapped. At one point, while cradling my singed arm, I looked over at the stove and imagined myself on top of it. I was too scared to flee.

Between Mother's yelling, the throbbing pain, and the fear of Mother's command, my mind became overwhelmed.

I wanted to disappear.

Then out of nowhere I saw and heard the kitchen clock. All sound seemed to halt except for the electric drone and the scraping sound of the faded orange-colored minute hand.

It read ten minutes to four.

My brain snapped awake. I focused all my attention on the timepiece. I turned my head to look at Mother, and yet was somehow able to tune her out. Her mouth continued to spew, but I didn't catch a single syllable. I looked down at my arm. The throbbing seemed to subside. With a weird, calming clarity, my mind kept repeating over and over, *Ten to four.* My brain spat out, "Ron comes home precisely at four. She never acts this bizarre when her boys are home. Time. Just buy time!"

I stared at the clock, Mother, the stove, then back at the clock. *Simple*, I informed myself. *You can do this!* In less than a second, I came up with a plan. *My plan.*

I looked back up at Mother and flipped on an internal switch just in time to hear her expel, "When I say move, you better move, mister. Now, I said, stand up."

Out of trained reflex, I obeyed. But then my own thoughts intervened. *Buy time!* I wasn't sure what to do as I struggled to stand up. I couldn't put any pressure on my wounded arm.

I didn't plan it. It was plain, stupid luck. I slipped; I fell. *I learned.*

With Mother booming over me, I finally rose but instead of, as trained, standing exactly three feet in front of her, I slipped my feet back a few inches. Then, without permission, I committed the ultimate crime. I spoke. With years of reacting without a thought, Mother struck me. But before she did, Mother had to adjust and take a half step forward.

I fell to the floor, struggled to get up several more times, and when I stood up, made sure I was a full step back. Then I spoke yet again, only to have Mother labor to strike me down. With each blow, I stole a peek at the precious clock. I tried to focus on the sound of the strained electric motor.

I got lucky again. With my heightened senses, I heard it. The distinctive click from the front doorknob being opened. Mother didn't seem to catch on. A full second later when the front door burst open, Mother definitely heard that. The blood instantly drained from her face. I knew Mother could never afford to expose the depths of her madness.

In a matter of seconds, I tumbled down the basement stairs. In the dark, I slowly, carefully put on my clothes. As I did, I couldn't stop shaking. My adrenaline became replaced with a cold fear. My chest began to heave. Barely able to stand, a waterfall of tears flowed. Then, for the first time, I purged. I vomited out years of ingesting Mother's toxic eruptions and Father's "one of these days" empty promises.

In the cold, darkened basement, I didn't outwardly reveal a victory smirk or let out a smile, but deep inside I felt a genuine sense of peace.

A few heartbeats later the sensation passed. A jolting pain from my throbbing arm replaced my solace. I looked down at my right arm. Dark red blisters began to form. I blew off some of the blacken, charred hairs. Then stupidly, believing I could cool the burns, I licked my arm. Out of painful reflex, I nearly hit my face.

I felt repulsive.

From upstairs I could hear Mother gush to my brother Ron. "Aren't *you* the most handsome Boy Scout?"

In my world, part of me wanted to let out my despair. But I was out of tears, and I was tired of sobbing over my ever-escalating pitiful situation. I took a few seconds to recompose myself, but my now fast-processing brain calmly stated, *If you can feel it, you're not dead. Which means you're alive. You beat her! You did it. You bought a few seconds of precious time, you thought for yourself.* You did it!

In the kitchen, Mother continued to lavish praise. "I bet *you're* the smartest boy in your troop! I'm so proud of you."

I looked down at my right arm, inspecting the bulging blisters from the palm of my hand down to the middle of my forearm. I wiggled my fingers, wincing from the shooting pain. Again, I took a deep breath, flushed out all the useless clutter from inside my head, and in a tranquil voice uttered, "All you need to do is think. Think ahead, think for *you*. No one's gonna help you. They all know, but it's up to *you*. If *you* can do it once, *you* can do it again. All you need to do is think for *you*."

Above me, in the upper world, Mother heaped on praise. "Do you even realize how special you are?"

I imagined Mother leaning down to pull Ron into her, like she lovingly did with me during that mere precious moment at the Russian River. "Do you know how smart you are?"

A few feet below, I flushed away the thread of a memory from a lifetime ago that would no longer do me any good. My mind then flashed to another endearing moment of us together sitting at the edge of a log, but I boxed away that memory as well. I refocused on what I needed to do. "*You* can do this. *Yes, you can, yes you* can. *You've* got to try." I sucked in the deepest breath I could hold. "And begin—"

I slowly raised my right arm in a pledge, just like I had in every Cub Scout meeting. With every inch, the pain was excruciating. I couldn't quit. When I reached the top, I spread the palm of my hand. I then made the V sign of the Scouts.

Seared tears dribbled down my face. "As God is my witness, from this moment on, I vow not to quit on *myself*. And that *I* will do anything, everything *I* can to survive."

Just over fifty years later, under a galaxy of God's stars I am amazed. As most things do, it took time, but my arm eventually healed.

Examining my past, as a young child, I *knew* that Wednesday afternoon when I was burned was a blessing of sorts. It empowered me. It gave me *something*—something that other folks may not apply or even discover until well into their adult years, when they encounter something unfortunate: a divorce, loss of a job, a serious medical situation, or loss of someone they hold dear. I simply had to learn at an earlier age.

That's it. That's all.

It was that same raw determination that gave me ideas of how to not starve, how to adapt to life-threatening situations as a child, to years later eventually landing me in the Air Force. It was that inner drive that got me through paratrooper jump school when literally hundreds of candidates quit on the very first day of the grueling monthlong course.

On the inside, before my Superman days, I had to flip an instantaneous switch and with laser-sharp vision find simple solutions to any and every set of multiple challenges. But like my future superpower, on the inside where no one could see, my vow made me more proactive and mentally stronger.

∞

As a sixty-year-old adult, I'm fully aware I wasn't supposed to have made it this far. Only a year and a half into foster care, as a very young teenager, a renowned child psychologist had the gall to boast—in front of my beloved social worker, my caring but bewildered veteran foster mother, and myself—that there was *no chance* for me. "Absolutely not a chance. He's not going to make it." He spilled that I was isolated for too long. That the abuse I endured was beyond extreme. I could never adapt within normal society. That I would most likely end up dead or in prison before I turned twenty.

A heartbeat later, Miss Gold, the kindest of all social workers, jabbed me in the side, and whispered, "Don't you listen to that crap. If *my* David can survive all that you have, without any help, well then, you can indeed do anything!"

Next to me, my foster mother, Mrs. Cantanz, challenged me. "We expect nothing but greatness from you. And never forget, you survived. We've *all* survived for a reason! Make it work for you."

I was exceptionally lucky. I was blessed. I knew that. And, in addition, I was always appreciative. Yet those who looked down at me, like Mother, never realized that I covertly worked. I diligently crawled on glass for my luck. I plowed through. Over, under, sideways, in any direction. Ignorantly, arrogantly, obtusely, I battled.

If Mother gave me any blessings, they were these two things. First: Never lower my guard. Stay vigilant in all things, at all times. Second: She made me want it more! To take nothing for granted. That I would have to work harder and endure more to accomplish the mere norm.

❧

Now, as a psychologically battered sixty-year-old, I must once again suit up, dig in, and fight. It's not fair. I feel I don't deserve this. I know it's going to be a grind. I'm scared that I don't have the strength, that I'm too worn, that I may not pull through. But if I try, it just might give me a thread of a chance. Which is far better than where I'm at in this part of my stagnant, vapid life.

It just may be a foothold, the footing to a better life. And just as I had discovered in the basement, I again may have a chance to find happiness from within.

Staring at my arm, I take in a deep breath. I feel clean. I can get through this rough patch of my life. *It's only for the now,* I inform myself. Through a series of twisted, unprecedented events, in the midst of calamity, I have a chance, a last chance of being blessed with a do-over.

I don't feel that instant, powerful surge as I did in the basement, but a tiny flicker. And that just might be enough.

CR

I stroll inside and turn off the TV that I use for background noise so that I don't feel completely alone. I ensure the front door is locked, then step into the former guest bedroom. I stare at a lifetime of belongings that will soon be put into storage. For how long, I truly don't know. I have never lived in such a void like this in my adult life. Before COVID, for me everything was one, two, three: precisely planned and followed through, right down the line, to the most minute detail.

In the guest bedroom, I become nervous. Hyper-overwhelmed. I have so much to accomplish in such a short amount of time, with far more important commitments in other areas. Then there are the endless plans, within more scenarios, for a home that I still have not acquired.

I see a box that needs to be moved. I place it on top of a stack of packed items. "That's it, ol' man," I playfully growl to myself. "One box at a time." As I lift the heavier box on top of a towering pile, it slips from my grasp. Before it hits the floor, possibly breaking the fragile contents, I suddenly scoop up the corner of the cardboard container, then gently replace it to the floor. But not before my right hand cushions the blow.

In the darkness, I inspect my hand just as I did years ago. I stretch the palm of my hand and twiddle my fingers. I then flip my palm downward, drop my elbow, and fully raise my arm upward. As it becomes vertical, I make the Cub Scout sign.

There is no searing pain. No waterfall of tears. I'm not a prisoner in a darkened, cold basement. In a calming voice, I vow, "One box at a time. One day at a time. You've endured worse. You can do *this*. It's gonna work out. Just keep pushing. Just keep it moving. You're just going through a rough patch. Nothing more, nothing less. Don't quit on yourself."

I remain still for a few extra seconds. I want my promise to resonate as it did when I was truly in jeopardy. I'm doing bad, but nothing like before. Before lowering my arm, I state, "You've got this! Now *begin*."

Chapter Seven
TURNING POINTS

I'M OUT OF TIME.

I tried to accomplish what I do best, Mission Impossible–style problem-solving while analyzing the exact core of the situation to find an unknown set of paths. Stay focused. Push through. Go over, under, sideways to find a way. I'm an expert at finding keys to impenetrable doors.

At least I felt I was, before my divorce. And before the sudden, explosive, unexpected loss of a relative.

Before existing in COVID World.

I lost.

I have no home to move in to—at least any place where I desire—that's close to my budget.

I've searched, scoured, and surfed the Web until my eyes felt Gorilla Super Glued. Once, out of late-night, playful online curiosity, I did find a cute townhome in Wahoo, Nebraska, but when I checked it a few days later, it was already scooped up.

Adjusting to COVID World has changed everything. In the workforce, as folks discover they can perform their duties easily from home, they've fled their four-by-four cubicles, selling their properties high and buying (in their view) low in more remote areas in the Northern California region. In California's case, with increasing taxes and end-of-the-world annual fires, coupled with decades of long droughts, a great many folks escaped, fleeing to other states by the hundreds of thousands per year.

In the Russian River area, where I desperately crave to reside, a home, without even being listed, instantly sold for $100,000 over the asking price.

Just over a year before the pandemic, Kay painfully informed me that she wanted a divorce. As her words spilled out, I slipped and lost my balance, nearly smashing my head on the lime-green countertop. After our long conversation, I stumbled to the bathroom to throw up. My head seemed to spin, trying to capture all that Kay said, how she said it, and the intent behind every word.

Yet as Kay had described her feelings, I knew them to be true. It was lots of little things. Tiny cracks in our marriage. As of late, when we were rarely together, there seemed an invisible wall between us. Because of my dwindling finances, our elaborate vacations became a thing of the past. While my body recovered from volleying back and forth between two separate fire districts, well over an hour away, I napped more in the afternoons rather than take our long walks. Truth be told, I didn't put in all the effort that I had in the past.

When I knew I had lost Kay, I instantly dug deep into primal survival mode. I drove down the coast from The Sea Ranch and looked at several small townhomes that were for sale among the towering redwood trees.

I had hoped to easily recapture a prize from my past.

⚭

In the late 1990s, before my books took off, I had lived a secluded, spartan life in one of the quaint townhomes. I was so proud. Before purchasing my very first home, I had pinched every penny. I went without. I practically starved myself, nibbling on French bread and yogurt no more than twice a day. At times when on the road, I slept in rental cars near the local airports, or in order to literally save a couple of bucks, I stayed in the basement floors of dingy motels. Over time, even though I had accumulated a small nest egg, I was terrified to pull the trigger. I didn't think I deserved to live in such beauty, literally just yards away from the vacation home where our then family stayed before everything turned terrifyingly insane. Where my father and I shared an unexpected private moment. Where my two brothers and I were inseparable, playing fort on a massive burned-out tree stump. Where Mommy . . .

As a kindergarten-age child, at the river, after Mommy drew me into her on that heavenly sunset, I enveloped a deepened serenity like never before. Then later, during my times in the basement, I would replay that moment countless instances, like a nonstop movie.

I would clamp my eyes shut, straining to capture the crisp, sweet smell of the trees as the branches swayed above Mommy and me. I believed I could capture Mommy's flower-scented hair.

That simple, maternal instant and an unexpected, rare moment with Father dominated, beyond the bounds of obsession, the course of my life.

I didn't realize how much the events had a hold on my existence until I was suddenly thrown away, like garbage, one early winter's evening when I was Mother's prisoner, just a mere three years before my parents separated.

It was late Saturday afternoon. From the basement, I could hear Mother tearing into Father about everything under the sun. How everything was his fault. How Father was never home. The lack of money. Things that she desired. How he could never understand how hard it was for her. How she was stuck at home, tied down, with *the kids*. How she was *stuck* with him. How miserable her life was. How her mother constantly dug into her, berating Mother about how she ran her home. How Mother would never be good enough to come close to Grandmother's demands. It was the same clattering ticker tape Mother had been telegraphing for years. It was all *Dad's* fault.

I barely paid attention. All I craved was to steal some sleep before being summoned to clean up after the family gobbled their dinner. After years of my parents' battle royal, I had become partially numb. I could only imagine my brothers, upstairs, lying on the floor, bellies on the carpet with their hands resting on their chins, zoned out in front of the TV. One of them, most likely Ron since he was the oldest, would probably lean forward to crank up the volume to drown out Mother's screeching complaints.

As much as I had wanted to escape through the safety of my dreams, I had somehow known the subject would turn to me. It always did.

From above, Father made a mistake. He dared to insert himself. "For the love of God, Roerva—I mean, Cathy—please, please, just please settle down. Hell's bells, the neighbors will hear you."

A heartbeat later Mother fired off, "Don't tell me what to do. No one does. Not you, my mother, no one. Not anymore. I don't need to take that from anybody. Never. Do I make myself *clear*?"

From below I cringed. I thought Mother only yelled at *me* in that manner. A full second later Mother got to the core of her torment. My brain became fully alert. "So, you really think *I* treat the boy bad? Well, do you?" I could imagine Mother tossing a swig down her throat, before jabbing a finger into Father's face. "You have no idea, no idea what It's like. For God's sakes, you're never here. How can you know? You never know what It's like, what It's like for *me*."

But I knew, like me, Father, too, was beaten. The years of combativeness had sucked the life out of him. His breathing seemed labored. His rare cough increasingly became deeper than ever. His once-mighty broad shoulders seemed shrunken and grossly slumped over. Over time and enduring countless explosive arguments, I sadly realized that Father had been reduced to Mother's puppet. Father, in a sense, was Mother's private prisoner, too.

No matter what Father said, did, or even did not state or perform, he was trapped in an explosive, emotional minefield.

There was an unexpected, eerie silence. I withdrew into myself all the more. When Mother retreated, when she didn't fire off a quick salvo, it was only because she would soon erupt like Mount Vesuvius.

I could envision Father attempting to try to make peace before things truly spun out of control. "All right. Let's all calm down. All I'm trying to say is no child, no child on earth deserves to live like that. For God's sakes, Roerva, you keep him in the basement like—like some zoo animal. I've seen you treat dogs better than—than you do the boy."

From the depths of the basement, I heard Mother slam her drink on the kitchen countertop. Father had crossed the unwritten, invisible line. And for that, *I* would have to pay the toll. Inside my head I began to spool up all the things Mother might do to me. But because it was late on the weekend afternoon and she hadn't begun cooking, and with the boys inside the house due to the fog-filled weather, I had instantly calculated it wouldn't be that bad.

But still, I had to prepare myself. It was all so draining. Every day. More taxing on the weekends. More so when Father was away. I felt so exhausted, so minuscule. I prayed I could somehow, magically, simply disappear.

I must have been distracted within my own pitiful wallow. I had somehow missed Mother's pounding strides from the kitchen, across the narrow hallway, to the basement door. From above, the door burst open. Heaving, Mother bellowed, "You! Ass up here! Now!"

In a matter of seconds, I stood in the kitchen, in front of both parents, shivering from fear and the still coldness from below. Just as Mother had wanted. As normal, I stood in the "position of address," hands glued to my sides, with my chin tilted down to my chest. Though my eyes were glued to the spotted floor, I sneaked a peek. Father stood lifeless, just an arm's length of a hug away, in front of me.

After grabbing my ear, Mother commanded, "Turn around. Look at *me*!" She then stared down Father as if to show off how much control she wielded. Mother then returned to me. "So, your father here thinks I treat you bad. What do *you* think?" There was a break followed by a long, infinity-like silence. I knew I was trapped, unsure what to say, what to do to somehow appease Mother. For me to someway wiggle out of another mind-numbing altercation was futile. I somehow knew it would only end up with me in excruciating, fainting pain with blood splattered on the floor, only to look up at my dazed statue of a father.

It just never ceased. It was all, all so constant.

This was my home.

Mother broke in. "Well, do I? Do I treat you bad? *Do* I?"

I simply wanted to die.

Mother applied more pressure on my ear, pulling me upward, forcing me to stand on my toes. Father seemed to lurch forward. "For the love of God, that's no way to treat the boy."

As if I were a hostage, with her free hand Mother stopped Father from getting closer to me. Her face was pulsating red. I nearly thought Mother would spew lava. "I don't need this. Stephen, if you think I'm treating It badly—well, then, It can get the hell out of my house!"

Another eerie silence filled the vacuum. Mother never acted in that manner before. Both parents seemed to stare each other down, looking to see who would blink or dare say something that might set off the powder keg. As always, I was in the middle.

In my mind, seconds seemed to drag just as they had that

Wednesday afternoon when I stole time. Again, I so wished to disappear as if I had never been born.

From above, I still heard Mother's strained breathing. I could only imagine her reddened, laser-intense, hate-consumed eyes boring into Father's overwhelmed, broken soul.

As bravely, heroically hard-core as Father was on duty, back home, Mother made sure she owned and controlled every aspect of *her* home.

For a fraction of a second, I thought I heard the strain of the faded minute hand from the grease-splattered kitchen clock. The pain from my ear had dissipated. I wanted to turn my head so my eyes could lock on to the timepiece—but I couldn't, due to Mother's grasp. I had so needed to connect myself with anything to take me away from Mother's madness.

Out of nowhere, Mother boomed, "That's it! Decision made!"

Before my stunned father could react, Mother squeezed the lower lobe of my ear even more as she half walked, half dragged me to the front door, with Father flailing a step behind us both.

With Mother's free hand on the doorknob, she snarled, "We're done. We're through. Get out! Get out of my house. No one here likes you. You're not one of us! You're not family. I don't want you! You're nothing! You're trash. You're garbage, and I am tossing you out! Consider yourself disposed of. You're of no use to me!

"I never loved you! I never cared. Never! This is not your home. Get the hell out of my house!"

Every word was like a white-hot dagger thrust deep into my heart. Had Mother not continued to clamp my ear, I would have collapsed on the floor, hugging myself in the protective fetal position.

Inside the deep recesses of my being, I screeched, *No! You did love me. You did. I know it. I used to—used to sing you Christmas songs in the summer. You said, that—that I could "croon a tune." That I was your special little guy. You held me at the river. We had a moment. Then later that next summer when we camped at the park, you—you picked me, me—to fish with you. Just you 'n' I.*

Not Ron, not Stan, you picked me! You held on to my belt as my feet dangled over the stream. The world stopped for us. . . . You loved me! I know you did!

Don't take, don't rip that away!

Yet part of me thought this was some twisted new game to see how far Mother could relish pushing Father. How far Mother could utilize me as her human pawn. Maybe she was trying to break me down further. Maybe she intended to further control both my father and my resistance simultaneously.

It was simply too much for me to try to process.

The push-pull tide of Mother's diabolical game was too much for my sleep-deprived brain and starved body to endure.

For a second my eyes met my father's.

"No!" he forcefully announced. "Stop it. That's enough. Stop the whole thing. Just let the boy be." As Father commanded his demands, I could clearly see his back and shoulders were stiffened with resolve.

Mother seemed to exhale. She let go of my throbbing ear. "No?" she asked in a sarcastic tone. As if not getting the response Mother sought, she switched.

Mother's fingers reached out to Father's arm, as if it were a lifeline, as if pleading. Her voice softened. It reminded me of Mommy from a lifetime ago. "Stephen, Stephen, Stephen—we would be better off with It gone from our lives. Think of the family. How many times have we talked about this? Cried over this, lost sleep over *this*?" Mother turned. With her free hand as if she held an invisible gun, Mother pointed dead center toward my bewildered face.

Mother stood beside Father as if they were one. Then as if cooing to a baby, Mother inquired, "How many times have you told me about 'the boy' this, 'the boy' that? 'The boy, the boy, the boy!' It's always about It. Stephen, you know It's the reason why we're not happy, why we don't—" Mother stopped. She then leaned into Father's ear as if to reveal a cherished, intimate secret.

Inside my head, I couldn't keep up. Suddenly my brain exploded with the obvious truth: *Oh my God, Mother's brainwashing Dad, saying that their lives would be carefree, so much better if I disappeared.*

Like me, Father seemed beyond stunned. His head shook. In a low but broken voice Father begged, beseeched the mother of his children. "No?" He seemed on the verge of tears as Father spread his hands as if to help plead his case. "This—*this* is *wrong*." Father appeared to want to say something, do something else, but it was as if whatever strength he had for me suddenly evaporated.

As if not able to penetrate Mother's hardened heart, Father sighed. He became more hunched over than ever. It was as if Father had aged years in front of my very own eyes. The last of his righteous energy spent, he choked, "All right, okay, I get it. Let's call your brother, Dan. He'll take in the boy for a few—"

"Absolutely not!" Mother sliced Father off. "It's no one's business. What happens in this house *stays* in this house! Period. End of story."

The front door unexpectedly popped open. I felt the cold rush of air rather than heard the sound. With one hand on the doorknob and the other on my shoulder, Mother bent down just inches from my face. Her breathing was still rapid, and Mother reeked of a combination of booze and sweat. "All right, Stephen, I'll leave it up to the boy."

I wanted to close my eyes, to turn away, yet Mother seemed to overpower me. Her bloodshot eyes were pure evil. In a slow, deliberate, grating tone she said, "If you think I treat you so badly, well, you can just pick up and leave."

I was simply inundated. My high-speed brain began to sputter. I couldn't get it to engage. To properly put all moves, then the countermoves, then the counter to the counter of another stream of more moves was all too much. I couldn't keep up to put the pieces in sync. I could not figure out if this was one of

Mother's new push-it-to-the-edge games.

I surmised the obvious: Mother was yelling at Father exactly as she did me, for my brothers to hear and not care. Demeaning Father about my state, then instantly, desperately pleading with him as if to lure him in. Her hand on the doorknob, opened the door ever so slightly more . . .

My eyes pivoted from the door, then back to Mother's face. Her eyes divulged this was no test. Mother's demand was real.

Run, my brain calmly stated. *Run!*

In blinding, rapid-fire shots, my mind replayed the hundreds of times I had planned multiple elaborate escapes, but the cold reality of the *where* to go, how to exist, kept me as Mother's prisoner.

Run! I told myself. *You can do this. Don't think, just do. Just leave.*

I was so worn out, but my vision seemed to sharpen. I stared at my worn shoes above the carpet that I had vacuumed hundreds of times for the family. My ears caught the blaring sound of the nearby television sets. From outside, a car chugged up the street.

Outside—out—get out! Run! my inner voice picked up.

Mother broke my concentration. "He won't leave. It hasn't the guts to go. He's worthless. He's weak. It can't do a damn thing for itself."

Even though I heard Mother and I fully knew that she was trying to break me, her words were like pings on my worn, battle-scarred, but still bulletproof inner armor. I had flipped a switch. Another voice took hold. *As God is your witness, from this moment on you will not quit on yourself. You will do anything, everything you can to survive. Now—you begin!*

I felt my body move. I smiled on the inside with an unexpected rush of warmth as my feet stepped through the threshold of the door. *Oh my God, this is happening!* my mind confirmed. *Don't stop! You've got this.*

Mother broke my trance. "There, Stephen, see? It's his decision. I didn't force him. Remember that I didn't lay a hand on that child, I didn't force him. Not one bit."

With both feet out the door of Mother's house and with my back turned against my parents, I had somehow felt as if I were floating. Once past the door, I expected Mother to reach out and jerk me back inside. With every step I moved faster down the outside reddened block steps. From behind me, I picked up the strained sound of Mother and Father as if they were exasperated while leaning on top of each other. In a sorrowful voice Father uttered, "This is wrong."

Instantly Mother salvoed back. "Remember, it was the boy's decision. Besides," Mother cackled, "he'll be back. The boy has nowhere else to go."

As I reached the base of the steps, I had so badly wanted to look upward at what I was sure were my parents' befuddled faces. With Mother's last dig echoing in my head, I took more control of my actions. Nowhere to go? I said to myself. *The hell you say!*

As I broke into a run up the inclined street, I knew exactly where I was going!

Out of all the plans I had schemed in the bottom of the basement—from how to steal food to how to absorb Mother's attacks—escaping to the Russian River was beyond elaborate. My challenge was how to get there and, more importantly, where was the river? I had known the town's name started with a G, and it was at the Russian River, but other than that, I was lost.

In the "comfort" of the basement, it had all, in my fantasy world, made sense. I just had to fill in a few pieces. Since I had known the river was north of the Golden Gate Bridge, so as not to be spotted I had planned to somehow crawl under the orange trestles of the world-famous span. Other than that, I was completely clueless on how to arrive at my sanctuary. But once I got to the Russian River, I would happily live under the worn, rumbling, single-lane Parker truss bridge. I would live high on the hog, gorging my belly on hard salami and fresh warm French bread, like Father used to feed the three of his boys at the vacation home.

I had even conjured becoming one of the umbrella boys working at Johnson's Beach, directly below the faded green bridge during the summertime. I'd help set up the folding chairs and stake the umbrellas deep into the beach sand for the seasonal tourists! I had it all figured out—kind of.

In the reality of the bone-chilling fog, as darkness took over, I looked down at my worn, threadbare pants, tattered long-sleeved shirt, and hole-filled tennis shoes that showed the holes in my socks.

The adrenaline from fleeing Mother's house had drained away. As the fog became a thick drizzle, I had begun to doubt my cherished plan. I had stopped to catch my breath, to think: What was I to do? *Come on,* I lectured myself. *Crawl under a bridge, really? You don't know the name of the town, how far away it is. You have no money, no scraps of food. You have nothing! You can't do this. You can't, you won't make it!* My chest began to tighten. My belly ached. *You'll end up as roadkill. You'll be on the side of the road. No one will know. You will die!*

I turned backward, toward the house. Mother's house. I shivered from the cold. My brain fed me: *At least you have a roof. You have rags to warm you. You have an army cot. It's not like you're sleeping on the concrete floor—at least. . . .*

In the midst of my despair, as if divine intervention from the Almighty, I smelled the distinctive scent of wood burning from a nearby home's fireplace. Of all things, I had so loved the smell of burning wood. It always made me feel warm. It was a blanket of better times that I had used to wrap myself, in a sense, whenever I felt alone and worthless. Yet above all things, it reminded me how, at the end of a long, adventure-filled day at our family's vacation home, Mother would light a firepit and, with cupped hands, swirl the smoke into our faces. Before drifting off to sleep, I'd bury my nose in my nightshirt to recapture the fragrant scent.

Don't quit. Don't quit on yourself, I instructed. You can survive. You don't deserve *her.* As I watched the gray smoke ashes settle, I thought back about the midnight rants that went on for hours. The impossible time limits on chores, even after Mother had bent my fingers backward. How she forced me to jam my finger down my throat, vomiting to prove I hadn't stolen any food that day at school. Or the worst pain ever, crawling on all fours after Mother would strike me with a broom handle directly behind my knees, over and over again.

"No!" I growled out loud to myself. "I'd rather die."

I took in a lungful of smoke-filled courage while staring at the twin set of red blinking lights from the distant towers of the Golden Gate Bridge. I instantly planned that I could sleep behind the bushes of my childhood favorite waterfall, Rainbow Falls at the nearby Golden Gate Park, which was only a few miles away. With any luck, I could hitchhike my way to the river. *But,* I stoically vowed, *I ain't ever going back!*

രു

As a gray-haired adult, I snicker at my bold, foolhardy, Huck Finn–like misadventure.

I only made it as far as a few miles before the police scooped me up and drove me to the station. From there I reluctantly coughed up Mother's phone number. A short time later, Father sheepishly arrived. Not the best poker player, Father stumbled with the farce that I had run away over a minuscule incident, of wanting to ride my bike—I had never owned (let alone) ridden a bike in my life. The officer then informed me how Mother was sick with worry. The final insult was when the policeman tapped me on the shoulder and lectured, "Treat your parents with dignity and respect. You don't know how lucky you are."

On the drive back to Mother's house, I had so wanted to capture the sight of the bright red blinking lights from the bridge's towers. To me, it was my beacon of hope that would someday, somehow lead me to my sanctuary.

Back in the stillness of the basement as Mother's prisoner, I reinforced myself to calmly flush out what I didn't know on how to find the river and replace it with what I did know. I learned not to become locked up and needlessly overly intimidated. I tried to break things down to the most minute elements, then take a chance of a single step that would lead me to another. I had to give myself the strength of venturing into the vast unknown.

◌◌

It took me another eight years, but I finally made it to the river. Truth be told, I confess to my adult self, it was simply a fluke. It was completely unexpected—a right-place, right-time moment in the course of one's life.

It was a nonplanned, nonanalyzed stroke of stupid, run-of-the-mill luck. In a sense, this absolute blessing reinvigorated me at the perfect time of my life: a much-needed portal that I felt safe enough, that enabled me to be wise enough, to step out of my protective box and venture through.

I was eighteen. I was already five months past aging out of the protective foster care system that had given me so much. I pushed myself to work sixty-plus hours every week and only treated myself to the occasional movie, yet I was still broke. My beloved foster mother Alice Turnbough was kind enough to charge me only a few hundred for room and board, but my cheap car ate into my bank account with the constant need for repairs.

I was aware with every passing day that my time was quickly running out. I was treading on very thin ice. I was still desperately trying to enlist in the Air Force, but the selective recruiters were already beyond worn-out from me showing up on their doorstep several times a week, begging to enlist.

Feeling little to no forward momentum, coupled with the increasing pressures of what I would do with myself, I became beyond anxious, then terrified. It was the same choking sensation that seized me when I was to be alone with Mother that first weekend in March, before I was rescued.

With time quickly melting beneath my footing, I became internally more possessed of being alone and possibly homeless. Out of frustration, ignorance, or even arrogance, I had made a snap decision and stepped out of my own way. Without telling Mrs. Turnbough what I was suddenly doing and where I was going (I had felt as if I were somehow disrespecting her trust and overly protective care), I secretly did something for me. I took time for myself.

The night prior, maybe as part of my intensifying fear, I dreamed of the river. I saw in perfect clarity the mighty, thick brown-and-red-barked trees, the ever-so-gentle flowing green water, and the teal-blue sky. Within my vision, I sensed I could somehow smell the pure, sweet scent of the swaying overhead branches. I could hear the blue jays squawking as they dove and buzzed for food from the tree limbs. In my dream I felt completely safe. I was whole as I saw myself sitting on a bank of the river's beached rocks.

On the beach, I'd be safe. I could be still and allow my brain to settle. Maybe even switch off. Shut down. I could watch. Absorb. Relax. Receive. Take in an everyday blessing on which no price could be levied.

That next Sunday morning, as a teenager with limited funds and less fuel, I sputtered north in my rusted-out, orange-oxidized '65 Ford Mustang coupe. I was beyond excited. With every mile, I thought my heart would explode from my chest. I couldn't believe I was doing this! It wasn't safe. It wasn't logical. It was so not me!

And yet, I informed myself, it was about damn time!

As I crossed the Golden Gate Bridge, I found the marker on the left-hand side that read "44," my favorite number, on one of the mid-1930s Art Deco lampposts that I had discovered that precious summer when traveling to the river. I glowed as I had as a boundless child.

I was on track.

But with the increasing miles clicking away on my odometer while heading north on Highway 101, I became anxious. I mentally calculated my fuel versus my dollars. My nervous insecurity began to overtake me. I punched the steering wheel with every passing exit, berating myself that I somehow missed my turn, that I shouldn't go on. I questioned whether I should quit and simply turn around.

I was way out of my protective box.

With increasing pressure, I spewed how stupid I was. "You didn't plan this out. You have no reserve. You're an idiot, a complete fool. Why weren't you thinking? You'll never make it. You'll never find it! You're nothing but a stupid ass!"

Miles later, in the slow lane, believing I could somehow conserve some gas, I saw it: a bright green exit sign with smudged white lettering that read GUERNEVILLE ROAD. My heart skipped. Moments before I took the off-ramp, I saw the ancient, distinctive rotating E that indicated the Emporium department store. I instantly recognized the sign from the summer trip on my last day of kindergarten. Out of blind faith, I took the road that led from the shopping mall to sparse countryside. A short time later I came to a T intersection. A weathered sign stated Guerneville to the right. I was reliving history. I was taking the exact route my father had on my most cherished, favorite trip.

I cranked down my window to take in the sweet scent of spring. I stared at row after row of grapevines, just as I had as a child when I had pressed my nose against the window of our family's battered gray Impala station wagon. More than a decade later, I was still overtaken by the serene beauty.

When I drove by and rediscovered the purple T-Rex standing guard at the town's Pee-Wee Putt-Putt golf course, I simply beamed. Yet the magical moment for me was staring at the green 1920s-built Parker truss bridge. And, just as my father had, I honked my squealing horn before rumbling over the single-lane road. While I did, I strained to steal a glance downward at my cherished Johnson's Beach.

After cruising through the town's Main Street, without applying any thought I instantly found the hidden, hard left-hand turn for the road that led to the sacred vacation home. I drove at a snail's pace on the quiet, unkept, thick-duffed, layered, and narrow street. With every inch of my tires, I heard the distinctive crackling sounds of the redwoods' dried, broken branches. Upon finding the tiny home, it looked exactly as it had decades ago. I couldn't help becoming mesmerized. Standing outside I imagined the blackened river-stone fireplace. The copper art piece of a horse that hung over the fireplace's mantle that Ron had made for our then Uncle Hap, who owned the home and adored horses before he passed away. Or the kitchen on the left side, and how once my two brothers and I were giddily frantic to get the dinner dishes clean so the family could see the Disney movie *Bambi* at the nearby River Theater!

When I came across the mighty, gigantic tree stump, I began

to feel light-headed. After wiping away the endless, thick, rope-like vines, I found the footholds Ron, Stan, and I had covertly carved out so we could scamper up and then sit on top of our secret, super-duper tree fort.

Taking a moment, I stood studying the wide stump. I then gently pressed my hand into the thick green moss as if it were a long-lost, ancient religious monument.

For me, it was.

So many emotions began to swirl within me. My mind fired off the thousands of times I sat in the darkened basement, fantasizing about this exact moment. Of being outside. Finding peace. Standing, without any form of fear, while absorbing the sun's warm rays among a creation of nature.

A free man. My own person.

∞

As I turned away from the tree fort and our family's former vacation home, I unexpectedly glanced down the street. Maybe because of my burdened emotional strain or another unexpected blessing from above, I thought I saw a sudden flash, followed by a long gust from the tops of the redwoods. A set of narrow beams seemed to penetrate the grove's towering trees. For a fraction of a mere split second, I saw him. I visualized my father standing in front of me, just as he had with his hand extended on that fateful summer day when we shared an unexpected bonding moment between just the two of us.

In my confused state, I gently muttered, "Dad?"

But the breeze instantly subsided, the sun's rays disappeared, and the moment passed. I stood staring down the narrow road, thinking about how the street somehow resembled my life. It reminded me of a passage of Scripture that in part states, "Enter through the narrow gate. Small is the gate and narrow the road that leads to life, and only a few find it."

Minutes later, after grabbing a few items at the town's Safeway supermarket, I quietly sat near the bank of Johnson's Beach. As I nibbled on a piece of thick salami stuffed between a torn-off section of fresh, warm French bread, I thought of Father. I thought of a home on the river. The two ideas suddenly merged into one.

Maybe, I mused, *if I could join the Air Force, I could send Mrs. Turnbough some money every month. Then when I got out, I'd have enough for a down payment for a home. Our home! For Father and me! I could get a job at the Safeway. Or find another job, any job! I'd find a way to make it happen. I just needed some* time—*three, four years max!*

My mind spoke in a clear but commanding tone: *Enter the narrow gate. The road that leads to life. Just find it!*

◌◌

Now, as an AARP-age, *seasoned* adult, after all the countless *Mission Impossible* calamities I've overcome, I know I can—that I *must* plow through to find a home. My home!

Throughout my life, I've always ventured down life's different paths. And somehow, some way, while the journey may have been fraught with peril, things have more than worked out. I just need to find a pathway that leads me there. Of all things, I have faith.

I only wish I had more time.

Chapter Eight
TIME IN OUR WORLD

"CONTROL 2, ALL NORTH COAST UNITS clear and available," my partner and good friend Captain Paul Plakos said to our dispatch, ending our late-night Code 3 call, which required the patient to be transported by helicopter. Always upbeat and chipper, Paul's voice seemed slightly dejected and spent. Paul and his wife, Bonnie, our fire chief, who also worked the local ambulance as an EMT, literally knew every soul on The Sea Ranch.

Over the many years and critical calls Paul and I have worked together, I can't imagine how such a genuinely kind person deals with so much intense exposure.

Years ago, when Paul was a fairly new firefighter, we worked with precision on my worst call, in which two young girls were trapped inside a fully involved structure fire. Upon driving the engine back to the station and putting the apparatus back in service, I think Paul and I simply gave each other a nod, signaling, *Good on you. Good job.*

After that intense call, I had given thought about attending the counseling services provided by the department, but within hours, I was on the road again to provide an in-service event back east. So as I had for many decades, I boxed up that event and stored it among the countless others.

"You okay, Pard?" I asked as I drove the fire district's brand-new behemoth of a fire engine ever so carefully down the pitch-black twisty road that leads to the coastal highway. "If you'd like to talk, I'm here for you. You can tell me anything. No judgment. What happens in the cab, stays in the cab. This is your safe place. You can trust me." I let the last line settle before going for the kill: "Well, maybe with me, you probably, most likely, really shouldn't. I'll go full TMZ: Maury Povich meets *National Enquirer!*"

Paul, being a brilliant psychotherapist and former marriage and family therapist, obviously knew I was simply jesting for a reaction. I got a smile out of him.

As I approached the intersection for the northbound turn, I gently applied just enough pressure to the air brakes, coming to a smooth stop. I then waited for my three-count, as in the past, small, souped-up, racelike, fast and furious cars have rocketed from behind, almost hitting our engines. "Clear left," I stated as required.

"And clear right," Paul announced, checking his side of the highway.

With all the different personalities of the various volunteers, Paul and I have a rhythm. While at times I can be gung-ho, "Aye, Moe," like the character Martin Riggs of *Lethal Weapon* fame, Paul is the smooth, far more mature personality of Roger Murdock. I was the excitable fuse while my partner was an even keel.

"So," Paul began in a slightly different tone. I knew what was coming. I eased off the accelerator just a tad to give us more time. "How you doing?"

With almost anyone else I would have instantly deflected the concern. I would have wiped it off with a simple "Okay," or deflected with some off-the-wall zany joke with one of my plethora of imitations.

But not with Paul. We had *our* rhythm. A quiet trust.

"It is what it is." Exhausted, I let out the thought of all that I still had to do in such a short amount of time. "I gotta tell ya, the last two years, I've packed over three hundred boxes. First for Kay, then all my stuff. That guest room is filled from floor to ceiling. I finally had to close the blinds so I don't have to look at it all. What it represents. Dismal failure.

"Such a needless loss.

"I really thought when we got our dream home—that we had fought so hard to acquire—we'd stay here forever. Together." I stopped before becoming overly sentimental. I felt a layer of detachment, just as I had in my years in foster care.

Just as I had painfully detached from my own brothers, it was during my time as a ward of the court that I learned not to get too close to anyone—from my loving foster parents to some of the kids I grew fond of in the homes to a rare classmate at school—as I moved around at times with little to no notice. Like other foster kids before me, I quickly learned to keep my meager but prized belongings wrapped in a tied-off pillowcase.

Once, while still new to foster care, I accidentally left behind my beloved baby red-ear turtle that I had worked so hard to save up for. I used to spend hours at night watching the little guy, with a lamp shining down, perched on top of his little plastic island beneath a bright green palm tree. Or taking my tiny pet outside where I watched him crawl on top of the blades of grass.

As an adult, it was hard to see crew members I flew with in the Air Force transfer out to other base assignments. Yet the worst was to unexpectedly learn of a fatal crash of a dear friend and former aircraft commander. Or an entire tanker crew of seven airmen who suddenly crashed just after takeoff.

The aircraft rolled past the point of no recovery in a matter of mere seconds.

As a firefighter, late one evening I was first on scene for a nearby neighbor. As I entered the home, the wife was frantic as she led me through the narrow-mazed hallways into the cluttered bedroom. My friend was cold to the touch, nonresponsive, and not breathing. I had to lower him to the floor and literally drag him to the entrance of the home so the army of incoming firefighters, medics, helicopter paramedics, and I could have enough spread-out room to work on him.

Next, I had to inform dispatch. I couldn't help but pant, "Control 2— 4412—at scene—elderly adult male, nonresponsive, continue all units, Code 3— recommend L.Z. [helicopter landing zone] at Sea Ranch golf course—coordinates to follow —beginning CPR."

Before I began chest compressions, I was already spent.

For more than an hour, a legion of us tried but could not revive my friend. That very same late afternoon, just hours before his passing, he had offered me one of his martinis. Just like the day I moved in, we'd stand outside by the roughened gray wooden fence railing. Without too many words, we'd both take in the heavenly, deep-teal-colored cove just as the sun set, at times causing a bright green, nuclear-explosion-like flash. "Next time," I had said. "We'll have one tomorrow!"

Then, as my luck would have it, the very next afternoon, I had to unexpectedly put down Kay's cherished cat, whom I had named Gatos. When the doctor told me it was way past her time and I needed to let go, I cried and blathered like a child. I couldn't help myself.

While petting the tired, matted, dying cat, I tried to instantly process my well of sorrow. Maybe it was my age? Getting tired of burying so much? Beginning to feel so worn out, or being overly exposed to others' suffering?

Of all the things I considered, I knew above all that I sincerely missed not being with my lovely bride, who lived ten-plus hours' driving time away, in the southern part of the state. Kay took a job, in part to enhance her retirement, help with some of the expenses, and to be close to her extensive family.

After Gatos fell asleep for the last time, I carefully drove her back to The Sea Ranch, in her favorite blanket on my lap. Once home, I buried Kay's cat outside where she liked to nap in the sun. As I did, I caught my friend's wife standing by the fence just beside the ocean's cliff, placing an empty martini glass on the post. We made eye contact as drizzling rain began to fall.

◌੪

Snapping out of my mini-trance, I stated, "You know, Paul, when Kay left, I should have just sold the bloody house and followed. I knew she felt too isolated up here, and that I loved the ranch more than her."

"Dave, from a former therapist, you have no idea how common that situation is up here," Paul related.

I nodded in agreement. "Sometimes it's like living on Mars." I quietly knew of an older firefighter whose wife loathed the over-seclusion of The Sea Ranch. She threatened to leave him if they didn't move. I highly advised the gentleman to yield, showing him my left hand that lacked my wedding band.

"So, Pelz," Paul continued, "just how long was Kay away before she—?"

Not wanting to hear the rest of the question as it was too painful, I jumped, "Five—five years."

"And you saw each other how many times a year?" Paul probed.

If it were anybody else, I would have told them to back off. But I knew what Paul was setting me up for, so I stumbled through. "She came up on summer vacations and Thanksgivings, and I drove down for her family Christmas party and spent a few days."

Paul quickly jumped in. "A few days? Then you'd drive back up to Sea Ranch, so you could quickly turn and spend the last three years working for Baxman at Monte Rio. Christmas, your birthday, New Year's Eve, and New Year's Day?"

"I know, I know, I know! I get it! You think I don't? I do!

"That's all I do when I'm not running calls at o-dark-hundred. I'm up. All night, for Christ's sake. I don't sleep. I can't escape it. All I do is think. Thinking, *I should have done this, should've said that.* I rip everything apart trying to sort through every frickin' aspect of my life, decades before I met *the* girl, why I act the way I do. I go through this e-v-e-r-y night."

"And?" Paul laid out. "How's that working for ya?"

In a mere matter of months, I had already concluded my folly while shivering outside in the late chilling evenings.

Without thinking, I blurted, "It was me. I had the affair."

Paul's mouth drops. "You *what*?"

"No, no, no. Not like that. But in a way, I did: Sea Ranch, Cal Fire, then Monte Rio, going out on any Strike Team, sometimes for weeks at a time. If not that, then every day I'd be at Cal Fire station or at North Fire station working, doing something, fixing something, anything, grudge work, vehicle inspections, hose testing that takes months in the frickin' hot sun. You name it, I did it.

"At first, I took those hard-core, specialty classes to become a solid firefighter. I was so into it! For me, it was all beyond cool! Then, when Kay left, it kept me busy and tired enough so I wouldn't miss her as much. At the end of the week, after spending five, six hours with Cal Fire, I'd drive down the hill and celebrate by having a glass of wine at the lodge, order some fries to go, drive home, watch the sunset, pray, warm up some leftovers, and go to bed. Simple-dimple! Then when she was here, I'd still respond, every call. . . . If anything, I abandoned my own wife. All the while, I really thought I could hold everything together."

I stopped my private confession with Paul.

"It was always *A few more years, and she'll be back.* Then a couple more, then one more year, and another, and she'd have enough to feel safe to retire. I felt like a prisoner at a parole board." I let out a deep, painful sigh. "I truly believed we'd make it. That we were different than other couples, that *we'd* pull through. Then we would have all the time in our world."

I felt myself tumbling down a hole. "I so loved being with that woman."

ଓ

But I knew, like most couples, what my fiancée—at the time—gave up when Kay moved in before the wedding. Kay quit her sterling career as the senior counselor at one of the nation's most decorated schools just a few years shy of full retirement. Kay sold *her* home that she adored, which was constantly filled with tides of people coming and going at all hours. The most wrenching was moving away from her teenage son, whom Kay protected and adored more than life itself.

Just so we could disappear into *our* world.

I recall a single thought just before Kay moved in: *I'm never going to have a bad day with her!*

Paul and I both became silent as the engine rumbled on the twisty black-void road of Highway 1.

"So," Paul gently asked, "do you really have to sell the place? It's definitely you. It's such a beautiful, peaceful home. You don't have to leave. You're a big part of this."

I shook my head in agreement. I knew exactly what Captain Plakos meant. Of all things, since my life in the basement, I have a strong desire to *feel*, to believe, that I belong. That I have a genuine sense of value. Being a part of the fire district team gave me a strong sense of purpose. That whatever I contribute, no matter how seemingly minute, it actually matters. That it might make a difference. Just as it did for me as a smelly child when a teacher would reach out with encouragement. Back then, I absorbed the single droplet of kindness like a dry sponge.

Hence, my duties gave me a sense of value: a strong, quiet, sincere sense of honor.

For nearly nine years, whenever a new firefighter completed their initial training, then were issued their own pager, in front of the entire crew I'd present that person with a nice T-shirt that read "Volunteer Firefighter," and proudly state, "Welcome to the family!"

The department, I reasoned—or more so justified—was why I clung on after the demise of my marriage.

"I know I stayed too long. I was thinking of leaving right after I shipped all of Kay's things. But then COVID hit, then there was fire season, then—" I trailed off.

"Dave," Paul interjected, "you of all people know, philosophically speaking, the world is always going to be on fire. There's always going to be *something*. What you have to start thinking, start implementing, is what's best for you. What's best for Dave?"

Paul stopped to allow me to process.

A few seconds passed before he chimed, "I gotta tell ya, Pelz, you took good care of her during the divorce. I don't know if I could have done all that you did."

"It was hard, but I had to. More for me than Kay."

I knew again where Paul was going.

What I kept inside was: I know *myself*. The vengeful swallow of every ounce of *my* pain, me. If I go *dark*, I know from experience—even though I've been the injured party—that if I retaliate at my level, it could overly maim the intended person, and I, in turn, will become consumed with pure hatred and revenge.

For decades, I've tried my best to walk the path of the high road. At times in my business and personal life, while slings and arrows were flung my way, I fought to be affable and simply press on. In the end, some people viewed my true intentions while others saw me as pathetically weak and a complete loser.

But inside, I knew in my heart what was true.

In the end, for me, all that mattered was focusing on keeping my side of the street clean.

"My dear friend," I shared with Paul. "I look at it *this* way. Kay is the kindest, funniest, most beautiful creature on this planet. I came from a dungeon. When I crawled out, I didn't speak the language. I had no currency. I so did not fit in! It was like I was from another world. And yet, I've been granted so much. More than anyone I know."

My voice faded slightly. I suddenly felt drained. "I've had

many loves. Me, geek boy extraordinaire! And I got to be with 'the girl'!"

Paul agreed. "Mrs. P was a hell of a gal."

"And Kay still is!" I commended.

I switched back to my initial reasoning. "Anyway, I stayed way too long. Like I said, I really was thinking of leaving when—"

"Frickin' COVID!" Paul blast.

In my best *Rain Man*, Raymond Babbitt voice, I dipped my head and cooed, "COVID sucks." I then jiggled the steering wheel. "Excellent driver—I am a most excellent driver. Yeah."

We both had a relieving moment before Paul asked, "So, why Guerneville? I mean, Healdsburg is so you. It's clean, lots of nice restaurants, bars, cigar shop, and more bars. Very upscale. Very Pelzer, Bond-esque. Or what about the Monterey area? You and Kay love Carmel—"

Even in the darkness, I'm sure my friend saw my quick glance.

Paul chuckled. "Oops. Yeah, I get it. But why go *back* to Guerneville? Isn't it kinda grungy? The floods, fire threats, the evacuations—come on, Pelz, you can do better."

It seemed everyone, from the volunteers, the Cal Fire personnel, and even my highly opinionated boss of the Monte Rio Fire District, Steve Baxman, was genuinely concerned about my choice of where to spend the remainder of my days.

"Didn't you live there before, at the village?" Paul probed.

"Yeah!" I smiled in the darkened cab.

"And you moved. You moved away for a reason. You can't go back, back to your past, it's not healthy. If you're going to move on, you gotta make a clean break," my good friend stressed with the best of intentions.

Like some teenager who dropped out of high school and wished to take a chance and move to the bright lights of a big city, I automatically responded, "It's not like that."

In my mind, I stated, *I've looked, scoured, prayed, and made every calculation.*

"It's not what you think," I said out loud.

Inside, I continued: *The times at Johnson's Beach, where I learned to swim, where I brought my son who learned to swim at the same beach. The super slide where my father took the three of us boys, where I took my Stephen, when he sat on my lap as we soared down on a thin potato sack. The village is literally next door to the home where Mommy hung Chinese lanterns, had us cook hot dogs on a whittled stick, where she'd tell us ghost stories before bedtime. It's where I felt—*

"I feel safe there, Paul," I confessed. "I can't sleep, 'cause I don't feel safe. Safe enough to unwind, to just let it all go. I'll feel safe there.

"Besides, it's for my Stephen and even more so for my grand-son, three—no four—generations at the river. I've really thought this through. Imagine, like you said, 'a clean break.' A whole new beginning. How cool is that?"

I smiled to myself. A private, wide, deep, warm smile.

What I did not, could not tell my friend or anyone else just yet was that I had just found it. I found a home. My new home.

Chapter Nine
PUSH THROUGH

LIKE MANY TURNING POINTS IN MY LIFE, my latest blessing came out of the blue—and luckily, within days of departing The Sea Ranch. Once again, just like my unexpected rescue in which I was instantly placed into emergency protective care, so much was happening at such intense speeds. Even as an adult, with decades of experience, it all seemed beyond my methodical, baby-steps influence. I had to make life-altering decisions much faster than I felt safe doing. As excited as I was, I was increasingly becoming chokingly terrified.

For me, many—much too many—what-ifs enveloped me. I hated being overly exposed so soon after my divorce. I felt nakedly vulnerable, encased in many unknowns.

Like my other major, life-altering challenges, I knew I had to do something to change the situation. I couldn't hold out for hope somewhere farther down the road. I was becoming spent by holding on with a one-more-couple-more-days, let's-see-what-happens-in-a-month-or-two, laissez-faire attitude.

And it all started by reassessing my plight.

ᏇᎡ

"Pelzer," Steve Baxman, at Monte Rio Fire Department began, "I worry 'bout you. What's your status?"

Sitting outside, sharing a bench with my boss was, for me, quite an experience. Steve was literally a legend within the area as he had served Monte Rio for well over fifty years. From delivering babies to seeing those he knew for a lifetime pass away, everyone knew "The Chief." As overly opinionated as he was, beneath that layer, Baxman genuinely cared. Above all, his humanity shone through. As we came to do when exchanging private, bonding moments on an old, worn bench, this time, I quietly stewed at myself.

The Zen-like Sea Ranch dream home now felt gutted. The peaceful resonance I had designed and kept up was stripped away. To me the house had become a glass-filled tomb. Yet out of respect for the new owners, and to the house itself, I not only left major items that I had designed for the unique home, but I also painstakingly spent dozens upon dozens of hours outside in the cold and, at times, pelting rain: planting, weeding, trimming, and pampering every inch of the oceanside perimeter.

Although I had given so many things away, I still had to move well over 160 boxes to a nearby storage facility. Luckily, since all I wore every day were my firefighter utility clothes, all that I basically had to load on my last day at the ranch were a few plants and the tortoise twins, with their wooden box shelter.

Even though I had rented two local cabins in the Russian River area, my lease ended on the last day of June. My buried inner stress was ratcheting up, knowing that after Memorial Day weekend, with the influx of summer tourists, the Russian River rentals would all be snapped up at a cost I could not afford.

One of my last options was to live outside the area, renting a room a month at a time at one of the low-end motels. But even that was expensive. Since the devastating Tubbs Fire of October 2017, and then folks fleeing the Bay Area to get away from COVID, anything that had to do with real estate, let alone a place to escape, was beyond insanity financially.

At times, to me it seemed something out of a desperate, apocalyptic, *Mad Max*–type horror movie.

I became so desperate for a place to settle, I checked out

the newest thing for mainly single folks starting out—or those like me, on the back nine of life—in the Northern California real estate market: the micro apartment, *homes*. Before seeing the unit with my own eyes, my initial idea was, I could suck it up and live there while keeping it barren until a particular village townhouse came on the market. Then I could sell the micro-place and flip that money for my Guerneville home. Simple!

Or so I calculated, in one of my many early hours, insomnia-driven problem-solving sessions.

But the only currently available rectangular-shaped unit was just over 600 square feet. It had a twin-size bed that folded into a wall, for mere dollars under $300,000. The agent seemed most proud to state that this particular apartment's only window measured a gargantuan three-by-two feet, with a dramatic view of the nearby bustling highway. When I asked if there were other units, maybe one that had more than one window, the young man scoffed. "Come on, why would anyone need more than one window?"

I instantly answered to myself. *'Cause I lived in a basement!*

The agent seemed to laugh more to himself. "Listen to me, this is perfect! All you do is get yourself a chair, a small nook table with a houseplant, and you're all set! I can even get you a discount at the local IKEA. I send them a lot of business. I can try an' get ya the friends-and-family discount. Trust me, in this market, with your budget, you're *not* going to get anything better."

Almost feeling the pull to cave in and submit to the situation, I began to think, *At least this is better than nothing.* So I pried, "Is there anything coming on the market with a view of the hills? Maybe something with a bigger window, without the highway?"

The young man seemed jubilant. "Anything's possible." Before I could inquire further, he lashed, "But of course *that* would be extra. A lot extra! And they're kinda hard to get. Gotta get in line, then we'd require a down payment, around 20, 25 percent. Lots of folks. Lotta interest."

"And a garage?" I asked, referring to the reinforced metal sheds.

"Extra!" the agent again proclaimed. He was then kind enough to inform me that there was a clubhouse, a "social room" with lots of windows, where I could watch shows on their huge new thirty-two-inch flat-screen TV and play board games with the other residents. "Free of charge."

"Free?" I pushed back.

"Well, let's say it's all covered in your HOA"—the monthly homeowners' association dues.

When I viewed the paperwork he reluctantly gave me, I almost gasped. The dues alone were well over 30 percent of my allotted monthly budget. It all seemed bewildering. I felt like I was some lost, out-of-time, broken character who had accidentally woken up within the series *The Twilight Zone.*

The agent must have sensed my apprehension. "Listen. I've been in this business for quite a while! I know what I'm doing. You're never gonna find a betta deal! These units are only going to go up in value. Trust me, the days of the two-story house with the white picket fence are long, long gone. It's a different world out here."

I tried to absorb the young man's pitch. The part he stated was true about the massive shift in elements and events, but I began to become triggered by the arrogance of his aggressive push.

At the end of the day, I didn't see myself being happy or feeling safe in such a closed-in shoebox. Toward the end of my life's journey, after all I'd been through, I just didn't want to settle, as I had countless times, trying to fix things or suck it up while hoping for something better to fall into my lap.

I must have strained the agent's patience. He aggressively cleared his throat. "So, you've been here for—ah—nearly half an hour. I've answered your questions. So, wanna start the paperwork? If not, I've got other buyers who are serious. Again, I've been at this for a while. I know!"

I almost asked the agent how old he was. But better yet, I scanned the young man's battered shoes and thin, worn, rumpled shirt with his scruffy hair. Instead, I simply stated, "You've still got spots!"

After baffling the agent with my ancient vernacular, I had to clear my head. I ambled outside.

I fully knew with every passing year that I became more ensconced in my own values. And in part because of my life's experiences, particularly my dark childhood, I viewed things through a different filter. I took little for granted. Small, everyday things meant the world to me. I prided myself on being thoughtful and open-minded, always thinking of others' perspectives. But folks like Mr. Real Estate burned my skin.

He had the exact attitude of a then-young, brand-new, first-day-on-the-job, don't-tell-me-how-to-do-things Monte Rio firefighter.

☙

It was a Monday morning.

While waiting outside the station for the 8 AM shift change, I briefed the oncoming engineer of my last day's calls, equipment, and apparatus service needs. A few minutes after eight, a car suddenly came to a dramatic stop in front of the station's engine bays, thus blocking them if we received specific calls. A young man hopped out in civilian attire with an I-have-arrived smirk.

The engineer gave me a look as if giving me permission to state the obvious while the young man leaned against his car as if he were some Hollywood action star.

"What time does the eight o'clock shift start?" I inquired.

The kid named Joe shrugged his shoulders with disdain. "What's the prob? It's only a little after eight. It's all good."

I calmly stated, "No, sir, it's not. And it's eight-fourteen."

"An' so?" young Joe grunted.

Anybody who knew me understood how much I respected the value of time, especially that of others. I was never late, and if anything was always extra early.

"What time do you guys get here?" the new firefighter genuinely asked.

Without hesitation, the on-shift engineer stated, "Seven!"

"Seven?" Joe exclaimed.

The engineer nodded. "Yep, and Pelz here, well, he comes in gear ready at six-thirty."

Joe's eyes flashed. He seemed to begin to understand what we were both gently conveying about the seriousness of this job. I lightened things up just a tad. "Six-thirty, plus or minus. I'm old, so it takes me a little more time. Seriously, you gotta be dressed and ready to roll out before eight in case we get toned out. And it will happen."

The young man smiled. He was getting it. If anything, I thought it wasn't all his fault. Someone like myself should have reached out to Joe on the particulars before he started on his first day.

Acting like some elderly statesman, I briefed Joe. "Okay, here's the ROEs." Before the young man could ask, I continued, "Rules of engagement. We're here to serve this community, save lives, and protect property. To be of true service to those in need. Anybody and everybody, with no judgment. You've got an opinion, save it for after the call. Never in front of those we're serving."

I let that settle before becoming deeply personal. "This is the best gig on the planet! But you need to understand, we'll see good folks, and some not doing so well, on their absolute worst day. Their very worst day. So we are entrusted to do all that we can, for as long as we can, for as many as we can. This is our silent credo. This is our duty!"

Young firefighter Joe's eyes widened. He was waking up. He was beginning to understand.

Even the engineer seemed affected as he never saw me in such fashion, the deep-down inner me. Duty, honor, country.

As the months passed, Hollywood Joe, as I dubbed him, settled in nicely. He was kind, worked well, worked hard, and most importantly, was receptive to pressing ahead in a totally different world of truly being of public service.

CR

Standing alone outside the micro-apartments, I instantly contemplated there was no comparison between the young firefighter and the pushy, commission-driven, blowhard salesman.

Truth, justice, the ol' American way! I stated to myself.

I exhaled some of my apprehension while capturing the humming of the constant stream of zooming cars on Highway 101.

My limp brain kept spinning. *My God, what have I reduced myself to? How could everything have gotten sooo out of whack for me?*

I nearly became consumed in another one of my self-induced pity parties when I saw a young Hispanic couple walk past me. The mother held the hand of an elementary school–age boy with thick black tousled hair. As the family walked by, the parents were kind enough to offer a nod hello. I felt an eerie sense that I had seen that child somewhere before, but for the life of me, I couldn't place him.

For a moment I was mentally paralyzed.

෪

I thought of my firefighter partner, whom I worked with on the dangerous Tubbs Fire, my dear friend Abel. He was proud and dedicated to his family, especially his ill parents and in-laws whom he lovingly took care of. If I was a hard-core firefighter, Able was an all-the-way family man. At times when we finished training, sometimes as late as 8 PM, he would drive nonstop south of Tijuana to pick up a relative when no one else stepped up to help out. Yet like so many other families that worked their tails off, for all his efforts, he couldn't seem to get ahead.

෪

A full second later, I snapped back to reality and nodded

with a smile at the family, making sure I offered a special gesture to the boy. Of all things, I didn't want them in any way to feel I was being disrespectful. I then studied the parents as they tiredly made their way to the sales office in hopes of obtaining the Great American Dream.

How in God's name are they going to make it? And how in heaven do they find the will to press on? I hammered to myself.

I couldn't help but continue to stare at the family as the zealous agent grandiosely flung open the door. Pointing his finger at the middle-aged man, the pimply faced broker proudly proclaimed, "Great to see ya. Have I got a deal for *you!*" The young man and I then locked eyes for a moment before he gave me a look to bug off.

☙

Still on the bench outside the worn Monte Rio fire station, I proclaimed, "Steve, it's absolutely insane out there!" Through our series of private talks, I knew Baxman was also surfing the real estate market since the massive Russian River flood a few years back. "Everyone's running around, everywhere, starving to find anything, just to escape. Then, as soon as something comes on the market . . .," I confirmed by a loud snap of my fingers, "*Bam!* It disappears faster than *Gone Girl!*"

"So your home in Sea Ranch is sold. The new owners are letting you stay there for a few weeks. Meanwhile, you're bouncing between there and a cabin here at the river, with no place to move into. And before the Fourth of July, you're basically homeless. Is that about right?" Steve jabbed.

"Quite the summation," I joshed. "Bet you worked on that all night, didn't you?"

Steve flashed his unique grin as he elbowed my side. "And there's *nothing* available?" Baxman sincerely followed.

I shook my head. "Nope. And the few times when something popped up, by the time I'd put things in order and drive down the coast, or get off shift here, I'd try to see the property, but it would already be sold."

"Which reminds me," Steve paused. "I never did see your Sea Ranch home listing. How'd you get it to sell so quick?"

I quickly explained the lightning-fast chain of events that led to the sudden sale, ending with "There was no need to list. The market's so hot, since the whole COVID thing, everything's—" I suddenly stopped myself, thinking deeply while articulating what I just blathered.

Ê©

That's it! I startled myself. *Everything's changed. By the time anything lists, duh, it's already sold!*

I tried to remain calm inside my head, but I was spinning too fast. *You keep chasing after the same damn thing, hoping for a different result!*

Stop. Stop it. Just stop!

Regroup. Rethink. Change the equation. Don't wait for a call. Don't wait on anyone. Take the initiative. Call them!

Nothing moves. Nothing changes unless you make the move to change. Just find a place before it's listed!

Ta-da! Simple solution, I chanted to myself. *You should know better. You should have seen it.*

ରେ

But I was simply, humanly overwhelmed with the barrage of nonstop, real-life events.

Ever since my divorce, after I had fought so hard to hold everything together for us as a dedicated couple, piece by piece, I felt stripped away.

Completely worthless.

My thick layers of inner protection that had worked for me during the darkest parts of my life were now a veiled ghost of my past. I had lost just about all self-confidence, leaving me feeling tired, weak, and vulnerably exposed. I had devolved to a fragile shell of who I once was. I had little to no confidence to draw from my inner well. I was not even a shadow of the person I had endeavored so hard to become.

And yet a flash of excitement surged through me. *Simple! You've got this!*

"Chief," I stood up and smiled, "I gotta make a quick phone call!"

As I scrolled my cell phone for my local agent's number, the insecure part of me screamed, *Don't bug them! They told you they'd call if something came up. They've told you they won't make a lot on the commission. You're pushing too hard. You're gonna blow it! You're gonna make them mad!*

I shut my phone off to breathe. I fought to rethink.

ଓଃ

By doing nothing, *I* allowed the situation to become dire. The days turned into months, and precious time had slipped away with no change—except for my increasing stress. Standing alone at the far end of the fire station, I gazed up at the backdrop of the endless rows of redwood trees. With my mind beginning to spool, I fought to be still. To just think it through. I remained focused on the forest of swaying treetops.

"This was it," I stated to myself. My come-to-Jesus moment. I needed to open up, take yet another chance, and entrust the two agents about the seriousness of my standing. I needed to sincerely ask for their help.

But I wasn't built for trust.

For me, asking for assistance was beyond my thought process. Something not in my toolbox. Too much of a vulnerable step.

In the past, while opening up, exposing myself—thus allowing others into my private, at-times dark world—I've been let down and violated countless times. There were critical situations when I fully knew I was being used for others' ends. Some, nothing short of sinister. For the most part I realized I was being taken advantage of, but instead of speaking up for myself for clarification or to correct the matter, I'd justify that I didn't want to rock the boat. I'd do practically anything to avoid enduring any and all confrontations. Even with mere disagreements, I feared all-or-nothing ultimatums. Or I felt that I somehow deserved to be mistreated—that I somehow brought it all upon myself.

I wanted to let people in, I wanted to be part of the norm, but it never seemed to work. And I never seemed to understand how or why the pattern always seemed to repeat itself. Until recently, during one of my late-night, outside, insomnia-fueled dissect-my-life sessions, I truly didn't accept how different I was compared to the world around me. Part of it, of course, stemmed from my past, the haunting feeling of being invisible, that my value as a person didn't matter. Then, while in foster care, I focused on surviving through nonstop work. I developed antisocial oddities.

As much as I could easily point the finger at others who I felt wronged me, three fingers were pointed at my own heart. In all matters, the obvious common denominator was *me*!

Many years ago, in a business matter, I confronted my then-hard-driving literary agent, who knew the history of my immense multiyear uphill battle to make the first two books bestsellers and the Atlas-like obstacles I overcame behind the scenes, because he embezzled my royalties for the third book. The man even had the gall to not only justify his swindling but stated it wasn't "personal," that he actually admired me! Besides, the agent seemed to boast, "You're damaged goods. You were doable."

For me, every aspect of my life boiled down to one finite element: the ability to feel safe.

Over the decades of enduring, then solving so many needless *Mission Impossible*–style obstacles for others, I just wanted to wash myself clean, do something for *me* while trusting all the time that someone had *my* back through thick or thin.

Throughout my life's journeys, I desperately craved safety in those I was supposed to believe in. It became a crusade of sorts. And like the fabled knights of King Arthur, it went on with no conclusion—a cross I constantly dragged around within my heart. It all seemed to stem not from my possessed, psycho mother, but from my once-beloved hero, who devolved into a broken soul, my father.

As much as I had worshipped Father, if anyone shattered my trust time and time again with empty promises of doing *something* when I needed help the most, it was Dad.

And now, while facing another critical challenge, I knew I desperately had to place my faith in others. But I was still extremely hesitant. I was reluctant because of my thread to Father. Because of his passing, I was never able to receive answers to why so many venomous, dire situations took place that he could have instantly solved. Yet the dark-heart part of me craved to unload onto him.

While still scanning the tree line, I could see myself finally confronting my parent.

> Did you, did you ever consider how much I prayed for you? Whenever you left for work, as I shivered in the basement, that I'd clasp my reddened, ammonia-soaked hands for you? Did you know how heartbroken I was when I'd stepped off the bus, got shoved around like some lost stray by swarms of people, only to go from bar to bar, to try to find you? And when I did, I'd have to help you stumble into some disgusting back room to take a piss. Then on the return trip, I cried so hard inside, I thought my heart would drown.
>
> When I joined the Air Force, I wrote you dozens of letters and tried to call your station with no response, not a single postcard, let alone a return call. I felt as if you had, once again, conveniently abandoned me. I didn't know if you were dead or alive. I'd beat myself up, wondering what I did wrong, like I did with her. That I did something that made you not have anything to do with me.
>
> Or, how later, when I started to save up some money, with every ounce of my entire being, in my childlike fantasy, for you and me to break away, to live till the end of days at the

river. And this was after, after all the pain, the degrading humiliation that at times I literally couldn't crawl away from, that I had to suffer, swallow, in your house, your madhouse, that you, in part, helped to create.

Every single day!

And don't act like you didn't know how bad it was. That she was simply disciplining "the boy." The whole "What did he do wrong now, Roerva" routine.

If I may, how did you two justify a five-year-old child banished to a basement? Sitting on top of my numbed hands while I starved, while you all, like lords of the manor, gorged yourselves? Then later, havin' me sleep, if you call that, on some moldy army cot? I didn't even get a blanket. Yet I have been informed that prisoners back in the day, even on Devil's Island, got a blanket or two.

My—God—you both must've been sooo thirsty the moment you deliberated your conclusions!

Then, just minutes after your bride stabbed me, I bled. I bled out, right in front of you, and you didn't do a damn thing, 'cept hide behind your flimsy paper, 'cause that was "your alone time." All you could do was cover your own ass an' say, "Better go back there and do those dishes. Don't wanna make her more upset, don't need any more hell in this house tonight. . . . Gosh, golly, gee, I won't even tell her you told, it will be our little secret, now scat, shoo now. Shoo!"

Did you know I had to clean up the blood, blot my own blood from your carpet? Why, hell no, how could you? You were doing da Dad thing outside with your boys, lighting their Fourth of July sparklers. Can't get any more degrading than that. But no, wait, we most certainly can! I nearly died of asphyxiation, right in friggin' front of you. I pounded and pounded and pounded that damn floor, inches from your work boots. Hell, you were still in uniform. We locked eyes. You saw me. I thought I was going to die right in front of you, an' all you could do was nothing. Nothin' except, "Jeez, Roerva, maybe if ya fed da boy, maybe he wouldn't steal so much."

When did you know? I've always wanted that answer. When was the moment you knew she was a psychopath and simply did nothing? Do you even remember?

Was it when I was in the third grade, when she had me throw up my hot-dog lunch when I came home from school, then hours later, after I did the dinner dishes, she had me eat it again in front of you with all that bile and saliva?

In the name of all that is holy, when did you check out?

What would it have taken for you to think about the mere possibility of doing *something*?

Or how about watching your Frankenstein's demented bride-from-hell choke me for—let's say thirty, forty, or forty-five frickin' seconds?

Do you know your eyes burn? As if they feel like they're on fire? Of course you do! You're a firefighter!

Could you have maybe stepped up if she didn't feed me for four, five, or how about seven days without a scrap of food? Not even from the bottom of those disgusting garbage cans that I used to scrounge from? Not a single—friggin'—crumb?

What did they used to call you? "The Bull"? "The Bull's got this. No one braver, no one stronger than The Bull. He saves women and children from burning buildings. Practically leaps over tall buildings in a single bound. He's da man!"

You put yourself out there as a firefighter, and I know what it's like. But you couldn't—you *wouldn't*—lift a finger to save me.

And here's another question I've always wanted to ask. That day in the rain, after you hugged your boys goodbye, when you limped over to the station wagon, did you know, did you see it? Was it deliberate?

Within my demented fantasy purge, I went a layer deeper, replaying that heart-wrenching Saturday in front of the fleabag motel on Skid Row when my parents separated. What no one knew, what I never shared with a soul, was my escape attempt!

I had schemed various escape fantasies since the first grade.

But at the very last second, just before I'd pull the psychological trigger, I'd always chicken out. As much as I justified that I had no money, was scared of where to get food, or knew no one to help me, the pure truth was that I was simply too weak to step outside my prison bubble.

While Mother presented Father with a cardboard box of his belongings, and while the boys danced around in the rain, my fidgety, frail, nervous left hand was grasping the cold, silver-colored door handle for dear life. Fully realizing that Father was permanently gone from home, I had no air in my lungs. I couldn't control my frantic breathing. I knew in my heart, *this was it*. It was indeed now or never. I could burst through the station wagon's door, flee down the opposite side of the street, and find an alley to cower in. With any luck, because of the pelting rain, after a few minutes they'd all give up on looking for me. If anything, maybe they wouldn't even bother?

Without meaning to, without overanalyzing my fate, my nervousness overrode my fear. By sheer, stupid luck, even with the beads of rain echoing from the roof of the battered vehicle, I heard the distinctive click sound and felt the pop of the door latch open. Not even a full second later, I leaned my body against the door. I sucked in a quick breath, ready to spring, when my passenger door suddenly shut.

In shock, I stared into the lifeless, nonblinking eyes of my unresponsive father.

> Was it deliberate? Was that what you truly intended?
>
> Did you know? Did you see me open the door? Did you see me trying to escape? Were you afraid to catch hell from her if I did? Or was it easier for you if I stayed trapped in her basement? To remain her prisoner till she disposed of me with you in the clear?
>
> Why didn't you just open the door? Why didn't you ever reach out? Why couldn't you take my hand like you did during that time at the river?

I could visualize myself bent over, gasping from being emotionally spent.

> She was sick. Completely, absolutely terminal. With all that I've done, with all that I've come to know, all that I've studied, I don't think, without a shred of doubt, anything, nor anyone, could have saved her. Mom was too far gone. No one, nothing could have saved my mother.

In the real world my chest tightens, but I have to make closure with my phantom past.

> I am sooo fricked up! Sooo broken. And, once again, alone. I could easily blame you and Mother, but it's me. It's all on me! I've been given so much, everything and even more. So many chances, so many possibilities, an' above all, I've been loved—and I simply just blew it. I gave away so much of myself. And now, more than ever, I hate myself for it. It never stops.

When I was married, I tried so hard, sooo much of quietly holding everything together for so long. But little by little, piece by piece, so much just slipped away. And now, I just wanna feel clean. I just want to feel safe. I pray just to escape through sleep.

I've screwed it all up. But I always tried to be, like you always said when I was small, when you tousled my hair before going off to work, a "good boy."

A caring person. A kind man. I always wanted to make you proud.

I named my son after you. He named his boy in part after me. I've always tried to be honorable.

I carried your badge, every step of my life. Every mission when I flew for the Air Force. When I served for weeks at Katrina, when I helped at Joplin, spent summers in Iraq, you name it. Dozens, hundreds of extreme ops, you were with me. The thousands of in-service trainings I did on child abuse prevention. Hell, meeting presidents, celebrities, you were with me. I still hold on to you, every call as a firefighter, hundreds of calls. Some pretty grim. You know what I mean. Hell, my own captain's helmet has your badge number: 1522. And now, on my hands and knees, I'm trying to find a place next to that old summer home, on the river.

I miss you. I miss how you smelled with your Old Spice cologne. How you looked with your shiny, thick, wavy, combed hair. How tall I felt when you called me "Tiger" as I stood beside you. I felt safe.

I haven't felt safe in years.

I lied when I told you that I found our place at the river. I'm sorry for that. I only had three, maybe four thousand bucks. I really wanted to get us a home. I thought it would solve things. Somehow make it all cleaner. One fresh swipe.

Now, in a small way, I'm trying for my Stephen, and his boy, S. J., you know, leave 'em something. A heritage thing! But after decades of doing for God, country, and whomever, I'm really doing this for me.

And after all the storms that I've brought upon myself, after stupidly, foolishly scrambling around, trying to make others over-the-moon ecstatic, at such a costly loss, now, after dissecting my life to the smallest of details, I truly believe that God is giving me a complete, final do-over. A blessed last chance.

I just need this break, a piece of luck—something.

In reality world, my brain sputtered. Yet I pushed through.

I just wish you of all people didn't shut me down. That you didn't shut that door on me. You saw my eyes, like you had so many times before. You must have felt me. My desperation. My life-and-death anxiety. I was real, just inches away. I mattered. I just prayed that you would simply reach out to me. It could have changed things. You could have saved me.

If only you would have reached out as you had for years upon years grudgingly promised: "One of these days."

All in all, if it were me, I would have opened that door.

In real life, a heartbeat later, a shock wave hit me. *David James Pelzer,* a calm voice instructed inside my head, *Enter— through the narrow gate. Small is the road that leads to life. Only a few find it.*

You're the few!

My chest tightened and I felt as if I had endured an epic marathon. I did all I could to keep it together. I prayed that the chief or any firefighter at the station wouldn't catch on to my inner strain.

I continued with my needed pep talk to myself. *This is your moment. All your experiences have brought you here, right now, for a reason. You've craved, you've prayed for a sign. With all the swirling chaos in this world, today, maybe God is trying to help you. Talking to you. Listen and receive. Open your heart, reach out, trust in* yourself.

"Open the door," I challenged.

"Okay," I confirmed under my breath. "Dave, just reach out. Open your own door. Step through and move on. Nothing moves unless you move it. Make the stupid phone call, explain the situation, and just ask for their help."

∞

Just like decades ago when I called the sergeant, days before I outprocessed with the Air Force, once again I was luckily blessed. My life unexpectedly, drastically changed for the better.

A few Saturdays later, I scanned The Sea Ranch dream house one last time. I was proud that I left the coveted home beyond spotless. Not a speck of dust anywhere. Everything was beyond pristine. Every piece of wooden furniture was heavily oiled. The outside spring flowers and indoor flowers were bright, fresh, and trimmed by my hand. I even gifted a pair of Baccarat wine glasses with a carafe and very nice bottle of wine to the new owners.

Outside I prayed, thanking God for allowing me to live in, to experience, such a unique, serene setting. I also said a prayer to where Gatos and my pet box turtle of nearly thirty years, Chuck, were laid to rest. I then glanced over to where I had planted a tree on behalf of S. J. I was immensely grateful that Stephen's family came up to spend the night before I sold the house. Between the three adults, we took hundreds of nonstop pictures, including one that Cyndel took of me holding S. J., with my son by my side, as we all gazed at thunderous waves just below us.

Finally, I stood behind the set of outside beach chairs, recalling the time I returned home after a serious call when Kay had just minutes earlier driven up for her summer vacation. It had, as always, taken me weeks to prep the home to the precise second of the arrival of my bride as if she were a dignitary of sorts.

To me, Kay always was.

And as always, I designed and planted two tall cascading orchids with orange impatiens at the base, with bright green moss inside a wide Japanese wooden bowl, and a large, carved-out redwood burl as a tribute to Kay and the serenity of our then-resortlike home.

When I stealthily returned home on that day, I stood behind Kay for several minutes. I studied her taking time for herself, taking in the majestic beauty. She had no idea. Kay delicately sipped from her glass of wine while gently resting in the rust-colored, cushioned chair. Rather than becoming caught up with the crashing waves, the squawking overhead seagulls, or the bright, lace-colored sky, I was transfixed by my wife's natural, graceful beauty.

I absorbed that simple moment.

Walking back into the home, as I closed the thick folding glass door, I was grateful I had taken the time to capture that memory.

Once inside again, I slowly did one last walk-through alone. I inspected every room. In the kitchen, I recalled the countless elaborate meals I cooked for Kay, as well as Stephen and Cyndel's favorite dish of green spaghetti. In the living room area,

I recalled little S. J. as he scooted on his padded behind on the wooden floor as he and I played with his set of toy cars. Then I smiled as I glanced at the L-shaped couch where an exhausted Kay would take an unexpected nap and where I held my grandson as we both watched the same cartoon movie Stephen and I used to enjoy when he was ever so small.

Another compounding sadness was studying where my beloved Steinway piano once stood. I never thought I'd ever own, let alone play on, such a beautiful piece of art. When I played the first four notes of a haunting song, appropriately titled "In Her Family," which I had heard countless times in over two decades, I cried. I couldn't believe I was really playing. I somehow felt I was unworthy of something I held so high. Before I made the purchase, I stunned the bewildered salesman by stating, "I don't deserve such a magnificent thing."

Yet for weeks, in every rare spare hour, I meticulously transcribed the letters of every note to various Pat Metheny songs, then practiced on the chords over and over with my right hand, then my left, until I slowly married the two. For a person with at times limited coordination skills, I was most proud.

If anything, the piano gave me solace. Whenever I left to travel on the road, the last thing I did before securing my home was say a quick prayer and play a song. When I returned, before I unpacked a single item, I'd sit on the bench and play. At night, the last thing I did was play a song or two after indulging in a few minutes of riffing, trying to merge some songs together.

It hurt my heart that the new owners weren't interested in the rare black-lacquered Dakota Jackson Steinway. I would have gladly *given* it to them. Instead, through the help of my overly kind friend Faviola, who helps me with my podcasts, she found a home for the Steinway. I donated it to a local school.

A few minutes after noon, after showing the new owners the particulars of their new home, I stepped outside, stopped, and offered a final prayer. I was beyond exhausted on every level of my being. With my energy draining away, I wanted to sit down and let out my pool of pent-up emotions after losing a dream home that I had thought my wife and I would live in forever.

But, like my basement days, I held fast. I had one final stop.

A few miles later I pulled into the unmanned North Fire Station, where I mostly responded when toned out for a call. As instructed by my chief, I turned in my Wild Land protective clothing, my pager, and my radio that designated me as a captain: 4412.

Standing over the table, looking at the neatly placed items, it took me a full minute to do something I had not done since the time I officially became a firefighter. I turned off my pager.

I then went into the wide-open bay to look at the various engines and the rescue vehicle I had driven during my time. In the background, various speakers crackled with ongoing dispatches within the tri-county area. I had somehow hoped before I left the coast that I'd get toned out one last time. I wanted to be of service with such a great crew, give them a good laugh, then take an everlasting picture together.

Another fantasy I held too tightly was staying on the ranch until my grandson was five. I planned to strap him in the front passenger seat, alone, as my father had with me. I'd have S. J. wear my "bunker" jacket while we'd simulate a call together. As Stephen and Cyndel knew that my time was short when they came to the ranch to visit, Stephen held his son in the front seat as I took them on a slow, creeping lap around the station.

I took another glance at the station. For a moment, not a peep squawked from the speakers. It was almost eerie that everything became suddenly still. I stared at the long row of racks laden with hung gear. As a sign of respect, I gave a quiet nod.

Since I kept my departure to myself, as it would have been too hard for me to say my goodbyes, I did something better. During our last training session together, I was granted permission to coin the dedicated, selfless volunteers. I explained the history of the coin, what it meant to armed service members, and how for over twenty years, with the honorary rank of chief, I had presented thousands of coins around the globe.

The last person I coined was a young lady who was brand-new as a firefighter. I didn't hesitate. With her father a fire captain himself—a bear-sized man with the biggest heart and, like me, a twisted sense of humor, whom I dubbed "Chuck-a-Soaris"—by her side, I instructed the firefighter to watch, absorb, and take to heart the movie *Saving Private Ryan*. I then took her palm, placing in her hand the heavy, glossy coin that displayed a bright American flag in the center. Around the edges, it read, "In Gratitude for Sacrifice with Honor."

Without a shred of arrogance, in tribute to those who have been of service, so "that others may live," since the beginning of time, and to those who had saved me, like Mr. Ziegler, who could have said this to me on my fateful rescue, I in turn commanded: "Earn this!"

The last thing I did before exiting the station, closing the heavy red door behind me, was to leave a sheet of paper at my designated rack. With my signature smiley face, I summed up my time of service in two words: "Thank you!"

છ

I then slowly departed The Sea Ranch. I opened the SUV's windows to take it all in one last time.

The sun was at my back.

Chapter Ten
STATE OF GRACE

THE FRESH MORNING SCENT from the grove of giant redwood trees fills my lungs. I can't take in enough. A light layer of fog quickly burns off as a sudden burst of the sun's rays pierce through the towering canopy of the swaying treetops that stretches well over a hundred feet above me.

Standing outside on my tiny second-story deck, I can't stop smiling—both outwardly for all the world to see, and more so from deep within.

I am beyond awe.

The house, *my* very own home, is beyond beautiful. Even with my extreme, meticulous planning, every item came together far more exquisitely than I ever imagined. And, like anything in life, it was not easy. The house itself needed so much work. From replacing worn, warped banisters; repairing holes in the walls; removing a dilapidated shelving unit that was bolted to the wall; replacing all the kitchen appliances, all the faucets, and all the blinds; removing musty, disgusting odors from closets; to repainting and adding carpeting to the ascending entrance stairs—the list was immense.

୧

In fact, when I first viewed the townhome, it resembled something out of some post-teenage trashed-out toga party.

Even though the home was one of the rare models I desired that had a larger, third-story upper bedroom, I initially turned it down. I feared the property needed too much work for me to put in. And a lot of small things irked me as well. My mind began to fill with a laundry list of all that it needed to put things in proper order. In addition, because of the various worldwide shortages partially caused by COVID, I knew there would be endless delays. I was hearing horror stories of basic everyday items, like wood or refrigerators, taking anywhere from six months or more to finally arrive.

With all the strain, struggle, and ratcheting turmoil around the globe, and the orbit of my own minuscule world, I fully knew I was being obsessionally selfish. I simply wanted something cleaner, easier—for me.

After initially viewing the unit, I stood outside frustrated. Without hesitation, I shook my head. No! That house wasn't for *me*. It didn't feel right. It needed too much work and would take forever to put in shape.

I didn't have the heart, but more so, the guts to inform the real estate agent, Pat, who went out of his way to show me the unit before it went on the market. I had to clear my head so I could practice what I would say to him. I very much wanted to let Pat down as easily as possible.

I strolled by my old unit, the only free-standing townhouse within the complex, that I had purchased twenty-five years ago. That's what I wanted. That's exactly what *I* desired, let alone (selfishly) expected!

Back then, when I had moved in, I literally had the house unpacked, cleaned, completely furnished, and fully operational in five days.

Back then, so much was seamlessly easier. Back in the day, a lot of things came easy to me. *Maybe too easy,* I mused to myself. Maybe I've become spoiled. Too self-gratifying, making things within my scope too instantaneous.

When I moved from the river to Southern California, the new house was basically turnkey furnished. Besides bringing towels, sheets, books, and clothes, the grand home was live-in ready. Then when I made the move to The Sea Ranch, I had the ocean home completely decked out, including three Asian garden areas bursting with freshly planted flowers in less than a week.

As I continued my walk around the riverside part of the Guerneville townhome complex, I recalled the times when young Stephen and I played Wiffle ball or laser tag, sometimes in the monsoonlike rainstorms. And before I'd drive him home after his summer vacation or weekend getaways, we'd play a round of catch, or we'd go for a quiet walk just outside the complex.

I craved to do the same with Stephen's son.

Becoming lost in thought while staring at the slow-moving green river, I surmised how the townhome I just viewed now appeared so small. It instantly reminded me of a few years back when I visited an Air Force base for midair refueling tankers. As part of the tour, a few air crew members showed me the newer version of the 1950s-built KC-135 Stratotanker. Once inside the tubular fuselage, it seemed so tiny, more cramped than it did a mere twenty-plus years ago.

David, I declared to myself, *maybe you are in fact overreaching?*

I stopped to give serious thought. A full second later I decided, *Definitely! It's who you are. It's who you've always been. It's why you've been able to do what you've set off to do. You dig, you claw, you burrow through. Your entire life, Mission Frickin'*

Pelzer Impossible! You own the narrow gate!

And, yes, maybe some things did come easy. But for the most part, you've crawled on shards of glass.

Twenty-five years ago, it all was such a different world. The internet was new and, for some, considered a fad. Amazon was known as a river. It was pre-9/11, pre-2008, pre-the-too-big-to-fail, take-all-the-bailout-money-and-run meltdown, pre-smart-phones and pre-1,000 channels on an HD, 3D, curved, flat-screen TV.

Hell, it was all before Kay.

Hell, as of a year ago, everything's different. Before COVID World. Deep within my heart, as I experienced firsthand as a first responder, then as I studied national and world events, I felt COVID would be with us for quite some time. Another year or more, and then some. Even with the recent hyper-rollout of the vaccinations, I somehow believed it wasn't going to be, as many expected, another flip-the-switch fix, like we had all come to know and, for many, even demand.

I picked up the slight trickling sound from the river's water. I began to relax from within. David, I told myself, *you, you of all people, keep reaching! If anyone can do it, if anybody can fix up that property with a fine-tooth comb and make it into a peaceful, stunning house it's—*

From behind, I was startled as Pat placed his hand on my shoulder. He let out a heartfelt, deep sigh. "Dave, I am sorry. I know it's nothing like you want. Unfortunately, the market's

changed. Everything's changed. I'm told it's only going to explode as a sellers' market, at the very least till the end of fall,
maybe longer. I've checked, and my partner's scoured, and
there's just nothing in the foreseeable future coming up in this
complex.

"You've boxed yourself in. And yes, I know back in the day,
there'd be five, six units for sale in here that would at times take
a year or more to sell. But that was before—"

"Frickin' COVID!" I interjected.

"Frickin' COVID," Pat agreed. "But hey, I've given it some
thought, a great deal of thought. And I say, get this place. It's
got good bones. A lot of what you don't like is superficial. I've
got this guy, a good handyman. He's crazy busy, super booked
up, but I can at least get him to rip out that shoddy bookcase
and that crappy sliding barn-door setup. I can get him to help.
Again, it's all superficial. I know what you like and how you
want it. I can help you. Trust me. I've got your back."

I gave Pat a wry smile. Without knowing, his words, "Trust
me, I can help, I've got your back," were like acid flung onto my
face. The last person who vowed that to me . . .

I quickly flushed the sensation before I could venture down
that ill-fated yellow-brick road. A blink of an eye later, I chuckled to myself. I was relieved by how quickly I was finally able to
let go of something that still punctured my heart.

"Pat, I trust you! You're a 'good sir.'" I then even half joshed that after I moved in, I could always snap up the exact unit I desired when it eventually came up for sale. All I'd have to do would be to walk over and carry a few boxes at a time.

Simple!

ભ

"Simple?" I openly questioned myself while still on my deck, peering into the main section of the townhome. It took more than seven months, multiple delays, hundreds of frustrating pull-my-hair-out-by-the-roots hours, with still no couch or a refrigerator that worked, but with every challenging obstacle, it somehow made me appreciate the final outcome all the more.

When it came to the endless boxes that I unpacked for the kitchen during a forty-eight-hour marathon, as my patience depleted and I felt overwhelmed by the lack of physical room for any more items, I'd stubbornly uttered my new mantra: "One box at a time, Dave. Just one more box!"

For me it made all the difference: to take an enormous task, chip away at it bit by bit, and somehow find a way to make things fit—even if it meant laying some dishes on their sides next to the stacked ones that only I would ever see.

ભ

From the deck, I walk inside and beam at the new wood fireplace. The immense unit almost cost me a finger when the person helping me install it lost his grip as he lowered the dolly way too fast. By sheer luck, at the very last second, I yanked my index finger away, before it became completely sliced off. The only casualty was my fingernail and a few sets of gauze.

To the left of me, between the Asian wooden dinner table and the deep black kitchen countertop, I gaze at a piece of art that I had not seen for nearly a decade: Claude Monet's *The Seine at Argenteuil*. Over the years I've studied and collected several reproductions of the French artist, but I had somehow stupidly not given a thought about my favorite art piece when I had made the move to The Sea Ranch. I had mistakenly left the painting at the local storage facility and completely forgotten about it.

With a child's ignorant mind, I simply liked the painting because it was immersed with my favorite color: teal, deep teal, and at the time I was always too busy to stop and absorb the artwork—how I could connect with the piece.

And now, some two-decades plus later, I stand in front of the painting and lose myself in its ever-so-romantic beauty.

For many, it appears to be a simple setting. To the left there is a dirt pathway, with a worn wooden fence on one side and scrubby plants on the other side. By the plants is the flowing Seine River, long and wide with a small sailboat toward the back. Above the river, a dark blue sky is filled with countless cotton ball–shaped clouds.

What I see, what I've finally opened up to discover in my own private world, is rejuvenation. On the left side, behind the fence, a cluster of tall green tree branches creates a canopy over the pathway. Because of the bright colors, I deduce, it must be spring. Lost within the painting, I also surmise that it is a Sunday, and with the clouds, mid- to late afternoon. I then look below the branches. I find the prize. I capture it. Something ever so simple, such an everyday thing, that I've overlooked dozens of times before. A couple, facing each other, with their sides toward the Seine.

The lady is wearing a white bonnet while the gentleman sports a black derbylike hat. To me, they appear to be holding hands. They are in love. Either the man has just proposed, or the wife has just announced that they are going to have a child.

As boats sail past, as folks stroll by and the clouds take over the warm late-weekend day, the couple becomes lost within their own world.

As much as my favorite Monet melts my heart, I am forever grateful during the course of my life to have had such precious moments in time.

In the midst of my Zen-filled townhouse, that unique Impressionist painting somehow fits in ever so perfectly.

It eases my heart.

I make my way past the kitchen area and into a small enclosed room. Years ago, when I owned the freestanding unit, I made that room into Stephen's preteen bedroom. On the side of the wall, I had a small desk set with his own set of collectable airplane cards from all over the world. He looked forward to receiving his special gift in the mail, just for him to tear open, once a month. The top of his desk was littered with an army of toys that Stephen had collected since before preschool. At the end of his twin-size bed, we'd sit scrunched together while playing video games on his then-advanced Atari 64.

But now I've pulled off something for myself that is beyond spectacular. I designed the comparable room in this home as a library of sorts. Upon entering, directly in front there are two amazing, unique pictures of an inflight SR-71. The one to the left shows the Blackbird in the pre-contact position, forty feet behind and slightly below the long refueling boom. The next picture displays the Lockheed spy plane in contact as fuel is being transferred while the two planes fly at 29,000 feet above Idaho's Salmon River.

On the adjacent wall, among a series of hangings, is brightly displayed the then-ultra-secret F-117 stealth fighter as it flew over the Persian Gulf after I topped the aircraft off with fuel during Operation Desert Storm. Below is a set of open shelves with more than one hundred books I've been collecting since my teen years on various aircraft, including a journal signed by the aircraft designer of my prized Lockheed SR-71 Blackbird, Kelly Johnson.

On the next wall behind a glass door resting on a hanger is my old, faded olive-green flight suit and flight jacket with my red-and-white-checkered silk scarf. Within the uniforms is Stephen's own tiny brown flight jacket he used to proudly wear while strutting around the house as if he were the great World War II fighter ace Chuck Yeager.

Directly above the enclosed area are stacks of carefully folded flags, proudly displayed, facing outward: flags that were flown on my behalf at the US Capitol, Mount Rushmore, and countless war zones, presented to me by service members from all over the globe, including a flag from a husband-and-wife team. After the lady landed her helo, the Special Forces gentleman quickly unfurled the flag and, in their words, "Got da hell outta Dodge before the fit hit da shan!" My most cherished one, which is encased in glass around a triangle-shaped cherrywood piece, was presented to me by Stephen when I gave the keynote address to his graduating police academy class.

To the right of the flight suit section, on a set of separate shelves under a soft set of lights, are a unique set of awards and a special torch. The first accolade is the Ten Outstanding Young Americans (TOYA) award. That award was presented to my childhood idols: President Kennedy, Walt Disney, Elvis Presley, Orson Welles, Chuck Yeager, and the actor Christopher Reeves, who played my beloved savior, Superman!

Standing upright in a separate enclosed section is the Olympic torch that I ran with for the Centennial Games. At its base is a heavy golden medallion given to me as the recipient of the National Jefferson Award. It's known as a lifetime achievement award and considered the Pulitzer Prize of public service. Other selectees have included Secretary of State Colin Powell and Supreme Court Justice Sandra Day O'Connor.

To the right, with gold-painted hands cradling a silver-colored world, is The Outstanding Young Person of the World (TOYP) award. One of the judges was my ultimate teenage hero of James Bond fame, Sir Roger Moore.

Beneath that section are two shelves. The top section displays some Air Force items: a piece of a Scud missile, one that was fired against our tanker base during the war (they were fired nightly), my slide rule, and an ancient checklist that still has Polaroid pictures embedded of a very young, beaming Stephen.

Below is my firefighter area, which includes various specialty tools I carried in my utility pants. Part of what I carried were medical scissors, pens, a notebook, a Leatherman tool set, two flashlights, four sets of medical gloves, and a pocket-sized IRPG booklet (an Incident Response Pocket Guide), in addition to a very worn, edge-tattered, folded picture of a smiling baby S. J. just before he sucks his thumb and a card from my then wife, scribing how proud she was of my firefighting efforts. At the front edge of the open section, after trotting the globe for over forty years, my father's badge is finally at rest beside my badge and volunteer fire captain ID.

Just up and to the right, in a second glass-enclosed section, is my firefighting bunker gear, otherwise known as turnouts. My personal protective equipment (PPE) is beyond out of service, because over the years it's been heavily used between the two fire districts. It took four separate washings to *almost* get rid of the stench of the mixed odors of smoke, water mixed with foam, mildew, and immense amounts of body sweat. Directly above the Febreze-scented gear is my battered red fire helmet. By its side, which I need to find the perfect frame for, is a slightly distorted photo taken of my last call, which took place in the middle of a cold evening after loading a patient onto a helicopter.

Hung on the wall beside my elaborately designed unit is my Firefighter of the Year award for The Sea Ranch. Still relatively new to the job, with just over two and a half years in service, when then-Chief Scott and then–Cal Fire Captain and dear friend, Shelley Spear, presented me with the accolade, without thinking I gushed, "I wish my father were here for *this*."

Below the award, on another beautiful wooden tablet, as a going-away gift, the plaque in part reads, "His Work as a Firefighter and Captain and His Daily Unwavering Dedication."

I muse, if a single word could truly describe the deep-down lockbox within a Fort Knox vault, "unwavering" seems to fit.

Yet with all the recognition I have been more than blessed to receive, I cherish the firefighter acceptance ones the most!

And while my library might appear over the top to some, I truly no longer have unlimited time left, nor the energy to care. I've decided, since the demise of my relationship with Kay, that I will no longer do or not do for the whims of others who have no inkling of what *every* item truly represents, and the enduring price paid. For every book, photo, knickknack, every single piece was designed to be displayed for only one person: my grandson, S. J.

∞

For decades—as I've presented leadership classes from the youngest of airman to the chiefs of the Air Force, and even in the grand historic setting of the Air Force Academy, to baby-faced, new, seasonal Cal Fire firefighters—I have proclaimed, "Live a grand adventure so to tell a great story!"

And now on the back part of the back nine of life, I have indeed *lived* so much.

Staring at the room, I am most proud. I let out a smile, something I seem to do more with complete ease as of late. I can only hope to personally relate and teach the significance, the heartfelt true meaning, of some of my ventures with my grandson.

I make my way up the final set of steps. At the top I take a right turn that leads to my bedroom. It's simple yet elegant and, most important to me, has an open, uncramped feeling.

Besides the king-size bed are four dark brown bookshelves that contain my set of James Bond tomes, as well as other authors who have had a profound effect on my life's journey: most importantly, John Steinbeck's *Of Mice and Men*. I've collected books as far back as my elementary school days when I desperately craved the need to escape. I even have a set of books that I once read to Stephen as he'd lay his head on my upper chest just before he would nod off to sleepy-time land.

I can now read them to his boy.

On top of the shelves are sparse framed pictures of Stephen and Cyndel's wedding day, Stephen and me, and of course a few of S. J. At the very end of the shelves, in a small black frame, is a beautiful picture of Stephen's mother, Patsy, smiling for all the world to see as she clutches our preschool-age towheaded boy sporting his beloved flight jacket.

At the far end of the room, the closet has been redesigned, including a set of soft-colored sliding doors. Out of the three of them, the one to the far right opens to reveal the most private of all possessions that I relish: sets upon sets of crisp, clean, scented and folded sheets.

Every evening, I rest on top of a soft, cloudlike mattress. On top of that is another three inches of filled feathers, with a gentle heating pad on top of it all. Just before I relax into a deep slumber, after reading my tattered Bible that holds decades of cards from my past, under a thick duvet and its beautiful cover, I lie over on what was Kay's side and recite my prayers. Then, just as I have since my days when I tried to keep my feet warm on the cot in the basement, I now warm them around my thick covering. Lastly, before I feel safe enough to submit to the end of the day, I wrap myself around a long, firm pillow.

I rest like a newborn child.

Staring at the bedroom, which endured months of painful delays from redoing the closet, the six-months' wait for the simple set of bookshelves and nearly not being able to get the thick mattress up the perpendicular staircase, somehow, like my past challenges, it made me appreciate the final outcome all the more.

"Indeed, it does!" I state to myself as I stop to take in the dark-red and gold leaves from the Japanese maple tree. The mature tree's wide leaves cover my long rectangular bay windows. It offers me a semblance of privacy, yet allows me another sanctum of serene, majestic solace in my own micro-world.

Nodding to the room, I turn and slowly stroll to the office loft.

I had the small rectangular area specially designed with a wraparound desk and enclosed shelves around all three sides. The desk faces the open loft. Directly above it, a wide skylight looms just above my head. During the day, I can see bright green branches from the mighty redwoods gently sway back and forth. At night, when working on a project, at times I can hear the pelting sounds of the heavy fog droplets. And just as I have in the corner of my bedroom, I have a set of tall, ascending, colorful plants.

On the side wall, in hues of black and white, are a montage of brown-framed pictures of Stephen and a few of him and me, from his toddler days until his late teen years. It took me well over four hours to measure and put everything in its proper order. At times, I spin my captain's chair to the left and simply gaze in delight at that boy's wide, beaming smile and the pure happy brightness of his eyes.

There are a pair of open shelves that are crammed with pictures. I usually prefer my settings with little to no clutter, but I couldn't help myself. Just above my desk are framed memories of Stephen and me when I returned from my last visit to Iraq, him and me when the Giants played in the World Series, the two of us sitting on top of Mount Rushmore, his first day of kindergarten, and him holding S. J. for his son's first official snapshot.

Behind my desk are pictures of my teachers. One in particular was taken on the twentieth anniversary of my rescue. There are a few more over the course of the years as I came back to visit them and worked at the various schools, juvenile halls, and some local colleges throughout the county. There's a special one of Mrs. Konstan and Mrs. Woodworth and myself the last time we were all together. Sadly, Mrs. K passed away years ago, suddenly, and Mrs. W moved into assisted living more than a decade ago.

There's a smiling photo of my then–tanker aircraft commander, Marty McGregor; my navigator, Dan Nollette; and myself, sporting the mid-eighties greased-up flattop hairstyle. By all our expressions, I remember firing some off-the-wall joke. Marty himself seems choked up in laughter.

As luck would have it, years later, on his first covert operational mission, Marty's U-2 aircraft broke apart. He was able to escape his jet but unfortunately drowned when he became entangled in his parachute.

Years ago, I heard the line from Ol' Blue Eyes, Frank Sinatra: "Growing old ain't for wimps!" And another: "I'm at the age where I go to more funerals than I do weddings, when God seems to take more than He gives."

෬

Death, since my childhood, has always swirled around me.

At the far corner of my desk, a tattered paper rests as a reminder. It reads in part, "Celebration of Life." I pick it up, connecting to a dreadful pain.

At times, when I still feel a tentacle of misery from my divorce begin to wrap itself around me, I quickly study a happiness-filled picture portal of my past. It truly makes me appreciate the sanctity of life. Because of recent events, with all that I've been exposed to, I have to be most extremely careful. I must be vigilant of my emotional states.

I don't want to end up like my relative who took his own life.

Out of respect, I say a quiet prayer. I then gently fold the announcement into a tiny square. I exhale deeply, recalling how I was almost pulled in—how I gave thought to ending my own life.

It was within weeks of lockdown from COVID. I was so tired and depressed. I had no energy. With each numbing day, I felt more like a zombie. I couldn't find rest, and once when I did, I dreamed my entire body was paralyzed. I could move my head to examine myself, but I couldn't scream to wake myself up.

After that, I was too scared of taking the chance of replaying that nightmare.

After beating myself up while staying outside late at night, I'd return inside, then lie in bed thinking of all the boxes I packed and shipped for Kay just before the lockdown. How I had painstakingly folded, then perfectly placed beautiful clothes that I had purchased for Kay over the years. I even stupidly, without thinking, packed several boxes of my wife's lingerie. The thought of my smiling, laughing Kay being with someone else was beyond any pain I had to swallow.

As days felt like months, my mood spiraled. I felt alone and frozen from within. Simultaneously, it seemed I was running calls to the same residences. I was seeing the same folks several times a week who only languished with each response. I didn't want to be *that* guy when my time came.

So I came up with a plan. A master plan, a Pelzer plan. A simple plan.

First, outwardly everything would be normal. The house would be clean, laundry done, outside flowers kept, and I'd add a few fresh flowers inside the home. I'd have the house unlocked, with the TV tuned to my easy-listening spa channel. In the kitchen, I would have cutting boards out, and everything set up as if I were about to cook one of my specialty dinners. In the corner section, on the kitchen countertop, as I had for years, I'd have my massive wine bottle opener lying next to a nice bottle of cabernet, but not too nice, as that might give my intention away.

Then, just before sunset, as I had countless times, I would stroll out to the fence by the cove, rest my glass on the wide post, then, as always, say a quick prayer, take one final gaze—and slip over the railing.

I thought about it for weeks. Refining pieces of my plan over and over, just as I had when I stole food as a child. I wouldn't say goodbye or gift anything away, and outwardly I'd still set off a few jokes when running serious calls. The isolation of COVID would be my cover.

But then out of nowhere, I received texts from folks I had not heard from in quite some time, asking me how I was doing. They said they were suddenly thinking of me, how I was on their prayer list. I even received a rare text from Stephen's busy wife with a set of happy faces. In a matter of hours, I was flooded with blankets of kindness.

The last saving grace came from my adult son. Stephen phoned. We chatted about the amazing world of being a father and how S. J. was scooting everywhere on his padded butt, grabbing everything in sight, followed by his distinctive, heart-filled, giggling laugh.

Out of nowhere, my son melted my heart. "I want you to be happy. You're a good person. You do so much, too much for everyone. Now it's your time for you."

We then reminisced about the day when I took young Stephen to Golden Gate Park. We started with the park's unique waterfalls, then we explored the meticulously kept Japanese Tea Garden, before ending up at the turn-of-the-century Steinhart Aquarium. And just as I had when I was his age, Stephen bounded up the thick concrete stairs and pushed himself through the heavy glass door. Panting from excitement, like myself at the time, my little big man rested his chest over the top of the brass fence while wrapping his long fingers around the seahorse-shaped part of the fence. Without a word, we both stared at the large, resting alligators and huge swimming turtles.

I became excited about sharing the experience with his family. Maybe too excited. "Let's not do it too early," Stephen suggested. "When the little dude's about five or six. We have time, Dad. We'll have time!"

Time! I announce to myself as I walk from the upper loft down to the main level. I stop in front of my roaring fireplace. I pop the handle upward, opening the thick glass door. I then utter two words before tossing the last known sign of the existence of my troubled relative into the intense red and orange crackling flames.

I escape my shame by returning up the staircase to the tranquility of my office. I sit and settle myself in my thick, high-back chair. I let out a deep sigh as I stare at my most precious set of private possessions.

My chest begins to tighten while my breathing increases. I struggle to perform one of my breathing exercises to help me relax by placing the tip of my tongue in the back of my mouth. *You're fine. You're safe. You're fine.*

I know this is all part of being exposed to so many levels of stress before COVID World, before my divorce, before joining the fire department, before Kay, before spending summers in Iraq, before spending weeks in the muck of Katrina, before any event or situation that transpired in my hyper-pace-filled life.

As I feel less faint, I chant, "*I'm* fine. *I'm* safe."

I begin to tear up, not from any form of disgrace, but a pure sense of relief—a deep, still feeling of joy. In front of me against the wall of my loft are two basically nondescript items. The first, encased in a lacquered brown frame, is a distorted, foggy picture of a gangly, long, faded gray horizontal log resting above a small flowing stream. To the left of my prized photo, encased in acrylic, rests a long sliver from the very tip of that ancient log.

The two items represent a simple memory that helped sustain me during my dark times alone in the basement.

During a family summer camping trip, through a series of events, Stan and I were left with Mother for a few hours. She had decided to go fishing, so automatically I assumed she would have Stan fish with her, as things had been dark for us for many years. Yet to my complete surprise, Mother chose me to be with her.

I couldn't believe my ears. It felt just like another cruel trick, like when she would have me perform the chore of doing the dinner dishes, then throw a plate of cold leftovers in front of me, then right before I could snatch a bite, she'd take it away, leaving me bewildered and still hungry, searching for the answer to "What did I do wrong?"

But it was real. Both Mother and I scooted to the very end of the sturdy log. With Stan below us complaining that Mom had the wrong kid, without a care in the world, my feet dangled just above the trickling pool of water. For a moment when I saw a fish, I must have leaned too far forward. For a split second, I could feel myself about to fall. But without my knowing, Mother had a strong grip around my pants belt. Out of scared reflex, I jerked my body backward, slamming myself against Mother's chest. I flinched, thinking of a possible reprisal. Without hesitation, my mommy cooed into my ears, "You're fine. You're safe. I've got you."

Even though Mother had one arm around my chest and whispered into my hungry ear, it was different. It was nothing like the sensation I felt during our time at the river when Mommy's hair tickled the side of my face, when I felt Mommy's heartbeat. But still it was a moment. *Our* moment. A mere beat or two. More than I ever expected at that time.

That simple experience has played out again and again, filling and reenergizing me when my well was beyond dry.

Within our world of hurt, for a flicker, we were both in a state of peace.

When I used to dream about Mother, in one instance we stood at the bank of the stream, both of us mesmerized upward toward the log. She begged if I could ever forgive her. Without hesitation, I responded with the correct heart-filled answer: "Yes. I have, too!"

Even as a preteen in the basement, after my parents separated, I somehow sensed that Mother didn't seem to have much of a chance. That her internal virus of hatred had killed her spirit and spread to the point that it consumed everything in its path.

As an adult, I fully know that my experiences, even the wrenching ones, were blessings of sorts. They made me appreciate the everyday, quiet, loving moments of life all the more. That the vaccine against injustice is indeed humanity.

Even in my basement days, it was always the simple gestures that sustained me: a compliment from Mr. Ziegler, an enveloping hug from Mrs. Woods, or a piece of bread from the school nurse. Then, while in foster care, the kindness of my providers, or a nod of approval from a stern Air Force recruiter. Decades later, before being dragged into a black pit of total despair, my own son's voice informing me he was thinking of *me*. Those nano-slices of life all somehow pulled me through.

Hopefully, I in turn—maybe, in some minute way—could, like countless others, as a first responder be able to begin to help cure others' suffering. That I can bring a semblance of peace to those who deserve it far more than myself.

Yet to do so, I have to continually strive to make my own life peaceful. If I do not forgive, I can never achieve the serenity I had fought so hard for and rightfully deserve.

☙

In the far corner of the loft rests a framed picture of the beloved Mrs. Pelzer moments after we were announced as husband and wife. And even though I've stared at the photograph countless times, I now study it like my precious Monet painting.

Wearing a stunning cream dress, with shiny highlighted shoulder-length hair, Kay was the epitome of *Mrs. Atomic Blond* meets *The Princess Bride*. Her sparkling light-blue eyes and beaming smile could have melted the camera lens. Like a giggly schoolgirl, Kay kicked up the river of white rose petals as we held hands striding toward our future.

Besides moments with my then-young Stephen, I had never seen anyone with such purity of happiness.

During my divorce, on a late Sunday evening, Kay and I were both very emotional about our loss. She sincerely cried, "Can you ever forgive me?" A sliver of me so wanted to lash out. To let her feel my pain, the shame, the sensation of being tossed away—like I felt years ago—for just a few seconds. Just a micro-flash of thermonuclear Dave.

In less than an instant, I blinked the dark sensation away.

Instead, I imagined myself with one arm around her shoulders, comforting Kay, with her leaning into me as if I was cradling her like a child, ever so slowly rocking back and forth. I could relieve Kay's heart-filled suffering. Put her on a peace-filled path. As much as I was deeply hurt, I would make Kay feel safe.

Outwardly, as Kay continued to sob deeply, I interrupted, "There is nothing to forgive. You just have to forgive yourself."

I learned since the passing of my relative that when it comes to judging others, before I take a speck of sawdust out from someone's eye, I first need to pay attention to the plank in my own eye.

⚘

After existing for years in a dark basement, I am now ensconced in my open, sun-drenched upper loft, where I take in a cascade of portals to my past. I have, just like in life, more beautiful memories than I do haunting ones.

"Lucky man!" I announce to myself.

Day by day, hour by hour, my inner heart is becoming at peace. The medicine of humanity pumps through my veins. I know it will still be a journey. But for now, I have time. Time for me to do as I choose, for myself. I have no idea what tomorrow may bring. But as always, with a little help from above, I'll figure it out. One box at a time. Come what may, all I can do is for the now. As challenges spring up, I will continue to walk through the narrow gate.

I will fear no evil.

For now, right now, I'm fine. I'm safe.

And, most importantly, within the confines of my soul, I'm *home.*

Epilogue
RESCUE DAY

FIRST FRIDAY OF MARCH 2022,
GUERNEVILLE, RUSSIAN RIVER, CALIFORNIA

STANDING OUTSIDE, IT IS CERTAINLY COLD. A thick mist escapes my heated exhale. I watch it float upward before it disappears inches in front of me. Swirls of white-gray, snow-colored fog lift beneath the thick, rich-green branches of the mighty redwood trees in my own private-grove world.

My worn, chapped fingertips are wrapped around an ancient coffee mug that displays its age with the darkened circular stains inside the cup and various embedded exterior cracks, the most obvious being the glued handle that I broke within a minute of my very first day of flight school. I was in my early twenties. I had thick dark-blond cropped hair, an overly unsure, nervous smile, and yet, from deep within, I knew I had what it took and more!

The world itself was all in front of me.

Out of all the countless items that will be gifted to my son, Stephen, and his wife, Cyndel, upon my departure—the awards, plaques, pictures, cigar humidors, historic books, fancy silk ties, decade-old plants, and whatever else they desire—I believe this simple coffee mug will be cherished the most. In black, bold lettering it states "SR-71." Below it in a distinctive outline is my beloved Blackbird, and beside it in scripted red it simply reads "3+," indicating the incredible speed of Mach 3 plus—well over 2,200 miles per hour.

Look, up in the sky! Faster than a speeding bullet . . .

Like some acquired archive from an Indiana Jones adventure, I gently place my precious mug on the cherry-stained ledge of my upper deck. I dip my head in prayer. I thank God, my teachers, the school staff, the kindly police officer, my foster parents, my angelic social worker, and literally everyone on the planet whom I've known, loved, served for, served with, or only merely met, who somehow, in some way, had an impact, no matter how minute, even for just a mere second, to assist me, protect me, or show me kindness during the course of my life.

In deep meditation, I also give respect to how many critical turning points I've been given in life. With time to myself to reflect, a clear head, and experienced maturity, I know I've made a gazillion mistakes, but from the deepest part of my heart, I fought to be my best, to be a good person, to pay it back and go way beyond paying it forward. For above all, especially as I become more seasoned, I value the sanctity of every single day as a unique blessing. And with that I carry a quiet specter of reality that I was not supposed to make it—and certainly not to the level of all the grand adventures I've experienced, when so many folks have endured and suffered so much.

And now, as I open my eyes and lift my head, I gaze while standing perfectly still on my upper deck. This is where I spend a majority of my free time. The branches of the mature Japanese maples are like a canopy over my head, and the cherry blossoms are coming into an early bloom.

I think of my father, the most broken person I've ever known. I recall my babbling lie to him on his deathbed. It still pulls on my heartstrings. Father, who was never there for me, but yet unknowingly drove me, inspired me with his very last words, as if pleading: "Live your life. Do what you have to do. Don't end up like me."

I let out a deep exhale from my past as I stare at the deck. Like most things in my life that I've painstakingly "fixed," the balcony replicates what I had envisioned in my fantasy lie to Father. Besides staining the dark upper ledge, I had, on my hands and knees, scrubbed and re-stained the deck itself. And as I had when I lived in Dubrava decades before, I have a pair of high-back director chairs with forest-green seats and backings. In its own corner proudly stands an intercontinental ballistic missile (ICBM)–shaped Fuego grill that has already been put to good use, grilling everything from thick steaks, "tented" with butter, rosemary, and garlic, to chunky marinated beef kabobs with an array of vegetables.

On different sides of the walls, I've attached two hanging bowl planters that I stuffed with my favorite, brightly colored impatiens mixed with shiny, long-stranded, stringy vines that sway in a gentle breeze. On another side of the one wall, for the first time in nearly a decade, because of strict HOA regulations, at The Sea Ranch, I now proudly fly my American flag. Even though the deck is small, everything is perfectly balanced without the feeling of being overcrowded.

Yet with all the items carefully micro-measured, placed, meticulously created, and admired, the standalone piece is a wind chime. It is bright red, made of bamboo, and given to me by Kay. Knowing my love for chimes, she kindly gave it to me as a Christmas present before I moved. As I knew how much Kay loved our then-beautiful Sea Ranch home, I didn't have the heart to inform her of my impending move. As I had un-wrapped the present and saw the box covering, I immediately stopped short of tearing through the box. I knew what it was. Like hoarding food years ago as a starving child, I waited for the precise moment to fully open Kay's present, only when my deck was pristinely completed. Out of a sort of long-lost romantic gesture, I hung the chime last and coated it with wood oil to give it a more glistening look.

As gleeful as I am to return to the river, I am still haunted by the demise of my former marriage. As much as I've dissected every aspect of my life, at the end of the day, my day, with whatever time I have remaining, like a passenger on a departing cruise ship after waving goodbye to those I've loved and painfully miss, I have to dedicate myself to step away from the stern, make my way to the bow, and move on with my life's journey. I will simply, quietly, sail off into the sunset.

I know Kay and I *truly* loved each other. I want to feel we always will. With Kay, I opened up and let someone in like no other. I literally trusted her with my life! But particularly in my case, with my life-forming childhood issues, hair triggers, and battle scars from decades of countless psychological wars, love was simply not enough. My executive director for my office for nearly twenty years, the beloved Mrs. C, recently stated just before my celebrated Rescue Day, "Dave, God loves you! You're great at saving the world and everyone in it, but you've got to let those missions go. You've got to work on saving yourself." She has preached the same mantra endless times, in various ways, warning me of my impending doom. But just as I taught myself as a child to survive, whenever I felt threatened, as a form of protection, I simply shut down. I did not, could not allow anything to penetrate my invisible force field.

And now, within my very own Fortress of Solitude, I can begin to receive Mrs. C's intention. It was and still remains hard medicine to ingest.

For me, some things take an extreme amount of time and energy to finally acquire.

But I've found that when I feel safe enough, for the most part, eventually I do come around. It's never in a huge, gigantic breakthrough, but from seemingly insignificant things. Yet, I **must** feel a level of security or even personal value.

Years ago, when I lived in the townhouse across the way, even though I had the rare luck of having three books simultaneously on the coveted bestseller list, I still hoarded my firewood, to the point that the home was near freezing in the winter months. Now, whenever I desire, I keep the fireplace ripping away.

Recently, when moving into the townhome, without thought I packed away the unique vases that I had only brought out when Kay came to visit. Then something strange happened. In a period of just over twenty-four hours, four separate people who came over to view the home all inquired, "Why? At your age, what are you saving yourself for? They're beautiful, they light up the home and make you happy! Why not use them?"

In my mind, out of habit, I had immediately fired off some dim-witted justification. But after relaxing for just a second or two, I shook my head in agreement. *Why the hell not?* I asked myself. Since that very day, my townhouse has been filled with bright blossoms.

I've always been of the belief that if two separate folks tell you the same thing, that's God talking. With four individuals, to me, that's God screaming for me to pay attention!

Yet for me, my biggest baby step was taking myself out to dinner on my birthday. I had planned it for some time and found excuses to nearly cancel my outing a dozen times more. I was proud to get all dressed up, sit at the rear corner of the bar, sip a drink, and people-watch. Rather than scurry away with my food to-go out of insecurity and habit, I slowly savored the rare indulgence for myself.

Why the hell not? I compliment myself as I look up at the light-gray smoke escape my chimney before walking back inside.

A few hours later, I make my way through a narrow path for my own private picnic. I shoulder a maroon wine pack that I purchased decades before but (of course) only used once. Like I had as a very scared young man when I rediscovered the Russian River, I nibble on a salami sandwich, but this time with chips and my favorite German beer.

I deliberately eat slowly. Between bites and sips I study the clear green river just a few feet below me. I can see for more than a mile the snakelike turns of the water. Even though the weather is still chilly, all around me dark-blue butterflies flutter in the air as if dancing. Above me, squirrels chirp as they run up the trees before springing from branch to branch. Blue jays squawk as they perch on the cherry blossoms that are days away from full bloom.

I become lost in the glorious splendor—so much so that when I check my watch, a full hour has passed. And I don't care. I've got work and other projects to complete, but I'm thinking tomorrow or maybe even the next day.

I take a final sip of my Spaten beer before I set off on my walk. I truly am living a different life in a unique world. My world.

My world is much slower, with little rush, and the tensions that can attach themselves to it.

I had no idea how stressed my body was with all that I was doing and going through the last three years while trying to begin again in a new home. As every room was unpacked and put together, I would become overwhelmed with emotion and sprint off to the bathroom. When the home was finally completed, I went to the bathroom six times in three hours. Yet after a few months, with each passing day I felt as if there were fewer stones in my psychological backpack.

I still have some tough days and my daily trials. But I'm trying hard not to take on too much. And at times when I do, I take a step back.

I still have my insomnia and I always will. I'm more than ever aware of my issues, but for the most part I own them and make them work for me. I am tired of guilting myself. I can't fret about tomorrow, for in this period of the world, "Tomorrow will worry about itself. Each day has enough trouble of its own."

Today of all days, I'm where I should be. Safe within myself.

I take a deep breath. I am excited by and yet reluctant about what I'm about to do.

Minutes later, I press my hand against a tired, worn tree stump where I first fell in love with the river. The summer of '66 was the most fun-filled and loving part of my childhood. It was the summer that Mother had taught my brothers and me to swim on our backs, where we spent our days at Johnson's Beach or in our hideaway tree-stump fort. It was also the summer when I spent a rare moment alone with Father.

I had no idea what I was thinking. But after my brothers and I finished washing the dinner dishes, I bolted through the open screen door and quietly followed in my father's footsteps, as he liked to be by himself with a cigarette after the day's events. Within seconds he heard me and, in a flash, spun around. I thought for sure I'd be scolded and ordered to return to the cabin. Yet without a word, Father smiled. I think he even extended his hand. And together, for just a few minutes, the world belonged to us.

Many years later, I took my Stephen on the same stroll when he was a very young boy. And soon, I will take S. J. and Stephen on that same path of life. It will be four generations of us, as I will carry my father's badge. I've already asked Cyndel to capture our moment with a photo. Perhaps that will become the heirloom piece above all others. It certainly will be for me.

As a family, I have no idea, with everyone's schedules and all the happenings of this different world, when we can make something so simple and yet so lovingly serene happen. As much as I long for the moment, I am quietly still. I have all the time in my world.

Perspectives

REVEREND RICHLEIGH HALE POWERS, PhD

It was a calming Indian summer, mid-October afternoon at The Sea Ranch on the beautiful North Sonoma, California, coast. My wife and I had recently relocated from Carlsbad, Southern California, with the intent to enter peaceful retirement.

Being blessed with a thirty-plus-year pastoral career as a chaplain focusing on marriage ministry, Spirit led me to The Sea Ranch Volunteer Fire Department. Upon meeting Cal Fire Captain Shelley Spear, I inquired if there was an opportunity to serve our community as a volunteer chaplain within the department. Captain Shelley replied there was not a present need for one, but would I be interested in becoming a volunteer firefighter? There was a meeting and a training session the following evening at the fire station where I could meet the troops and check out the possibilities.

The next evening during the training, I was tutored by an intriguing individual. Afterward, I asked Captain Shelley, "Who is this guy?" She replied, "Oh, that's Dave Pelzer. We refer to him as 'our firefighter on steroids.' You should get to know him; he'd be a great trainer for you."

And so began my journey with Captain Dave. As jokingly affable as he appeared, Pelzer was extremely serious about the responsibility of being a firefighter. He instructed me on navigation, radio communication, tactical response, position awareness, setting up landing zones for helicopters, the proper techniques of "squirting wet stuff on the red stuff," and a myriad of responsibilities, aspects, and nuances of what I might expect as a firefighter. It was an unending river of reality.

Like a pastor on his soapbox, Captain Dave always preached, "Safety, *safety*, SAFETY!" On one of my initial calls, as Pelzer drove Engine 4485 up a windy narrow road with another engine close behind, he gave me the assignment of "eyes of God." I was to look forward, left, right, and backward, constantly scanning for anything and everything until we arrived on scene and safely parked our mammoth engine.

"You gotta take in that everybody on the road is trying to kill you, so you're *always* on the defensive!" Pelzer lectured. A split second later a concrete truck came barreling down the hill. The driver slammed on his brakes as he careened toward us. For a moment, I knew the truck would hit us or we would spill over the vertical drop-off, just inches to our right, possibly taking out the engine behind us as well. I expected Captain Dave to hit his brakes, but as if piloting a jet, he simply eased off the gas and gently drifted the engine to the right. The concrete truck missed us by a matter of inches.

There is no doubt in my heart that Captain Dave saved us that day. He was cool and calm. He made it look simple. And yet on the most horrendous calls, I could see the deep humanity he had for others, for everyone. I always felt blessed when we ran calls together.

As a chaplain, it was heartbreaking to hear of his impending divorce. Few knew, but it leaked out. As we had the same beliefs in God, I approached Dave to inquire if I could help. He told me he was too ashamed to tell me. He seemed to age years in a matter of months. I gave him comfort and assured Dave he was in my prayers. It seemed to make a difference to give him something that he could cling to. And, as always, we hugged, and he sent me off with one of his grand salutes as he had hundreds of times over our years together.

I was sad to see Captain Dave depart from The Sea Ranch. He was the heart of the volunteers. But as if a blessing from God Himself, I got to be with Captain Dave on his last call. It was o-dark-hundred, bone-chillingly cold, and we had just loaded a critical patient onto a helicopter. Everyone beamed with smiles, some pointing at Da Man, our own cool-hand Luke.

I was happy to see Dave return to his beloved Russian River. In Scripture, rivers are powerful symbols of divine life, energy, and powers of God to nourish all life. Rivers have great meaning for spirituality, growth, health, and vitality.

The River of Spirituality is about laying down our egos, embracing that which often we cannot understand or have difficulty accepting, and with courage choosing to step into its flow and immerse ourselves in that water. Who knows what kind of healing and transformation may result? Acknowledge the sacredness of life, honor the sacred in all others, accept the twists and turns as tools for growth, and choose to step into the flow of the Now with peace, courage, wisdom, and hope.

Dave's entire life resembles the River of Spirituality. He has been a blessing to so many, and Brother Dave continues to be a blessing in my life's journey.

FAVIOLA AGUILAR

I am a young woman living in a small, close-knit rural area above The Sea Ranch area in Northern California. I first heard of Dave Pelzer's book *A Child Called "It"* while in high school, about fifteen years before meeting him in person. While reading Dave's book, I found that his courage and determination caused a weight to lift off my shoulders. For the longest time I thought my mother was wrong about the way my father treated her, but Dave's story made me feel lucky that I was not on the receiving end of such abuse. Ultimately it helped me feel like I was not alone.

Years later, a tragic event struck our community. Three boys, ages eighteen, seventeen, and fourteen, died in a tragic car crash. The world seemed so quiet the morning I found out; the coastal fog seemed to stick to the road. Those sweet, kind boys who I used to babysit were so young, so dear, and good young men with their lives mapped out for them—all extinguished in an instant. In our small coastal community, phones rang nonstop with the gut-wrenching news. It was something that hit our community very hard. In a small town where everyone knows everyone, it was a horrendous loss.

As a community, we were all grateful for the care and professional determination of our coastal firefighters who gave their all to cut through the crumpled car in their valiant efforts to save these boys and load the youngest one, still alive, into the specialized air ambulance.

Soon afterward, as we learned of the list of first responders, I heard the name *"Dave Peltzer."* For a split second, I made the possible connection but brushed it aside, as there was no way *that* Dave would be a firefighter, living in such an extreme remote area. Yet I remembered, in his many books, how he so admired his father as a firefighter and had joined the armed forces to become one.

Over time, there were numerous Dave sightings: autograph-
ing books at the small-town bookstore, interviews at the local
radio station, and increasing appearances of the tall, intense
firefighter.

I first met Dave in my new job as a local bartender. He was
rather elusive, quiet, and kept to himself. Some of the girls
at work would bring their books for Dave to sign, and a few
gushed like teenagers when they'd ask for a selfie with our local
celebrity.

It was the out-of-towners who were more hysterical about
sitting next to the famous author. But to us locals, he was simply
known as "Firefighter Dave."

For the most part, after duty, but still in his utility clothes,
Dave would come in, order a single drink and fries to go, then
promptly leave. He wasn't rude or overly curt, but I could tell
by the sincere expression whether he had a serious call or he
was simply deep in thought. One could easily tell that Dave
was always thinking.

Over time, Dave and I slowly started to chat. Knowing that
Dave had done internet radio for several years, including a
show live from Baghdad, Iraq, I carefully began to introduce the
idea of Dave hosting a podcast. Instantly I was shot down. He
seemed intimidated by the "fangled" technology, but more so
he stated how it would take too much time from his wife, Kay.

I was slightly taken aback. Here's this person who can easily
capture such an opportunity. I listened to some of his older

internet shows, and Dave had *it*: the soothing voice, quick wit, depth of subject matter, and above all, that genuine sincerity behind the microphone. I did my research and knew how he studied and admired the great ones, from Orson Welles to Edward R. Murrow to Garrison Keillor. With his notoriety, decades of public speaking, and zigzagging around the globe, to *me* a podcast seemed a perfect fit.

But if I learned anything quickly, it was not to have Dave feel he's being pushed in a corner. Period.

It took quite a long time, but eventually I broke down Mr. Pelzer's stubbornness. We began the long, grueling process of thinking about doing a show, the right show with a simple but substantial message. We conversed about him doing a one-man comedy-type show. Then we thought about one other person as a sidekick, as the straight person, while Dave would spew about topical situations in a lighthearted matter. Yet we both kept circling back to a self-help show: the hardest venue to break into.

But with Dave, everything is about time. How much time and energy he puts into things he truly believes in and loves. As much as, and I quote, "Pelzer is a firefighter on steroids," Dave was devoted to his son's family and, mostly, to his beautiful wife, Kay.

Because we'd get interrupted and get little done, we learned very quickly we couldn't do any work at any of the local cafés. So after assuring Dave I would guard his privacy, we agreed to meet at his place.

Like so many in the area, I had heard about the distinctive home. It was literally something out of a James Bond movie set. Upon walking in, I felt as if I were floating. Everything was pristine, in its proper place. The entire home was bright, open, and, in a word, relaxing. It was like a hidden resort that smelled like fresh fir. And then there were the flowers. Wherever I gazed, flowers of every type and color were everywhere: the kitchen, the living room, on the piano, and even in the bathroom.

From all the fresh flowers I figured it out. Kay was arriving the very next day.

After the quick tour, it was hard to reset and focus on our task at hand. My head was still spinning when Dave was toned out for a call. With the house unexpectedly left to myself, I had a rare chance to absorb some of Dave's inner sanctum.

Upon returning, Dave told me my uncle Abel, who also is a firefighter, said "Hello."

Coming from a big and at times loud Hispanic family, Uncle Abel is one of my favorite relatives. Abel, who is very reserved, told me that his best friend on the job was always Mr. Dave.

What a lot of people didn't know is that behind the scenes, Captain Pelzer took extraordinary care of my uncle and a host of other volunteers. My uncle works very hard and is extremely proud, and it's hard to pull information from him, but he told me that Mr. Dave had always helped by buying him hundreds of socks over the years, utility pants, and specialized firefighter gear. Dave made my uncle feel like he truly mattered and gave him a strong sense of value.

They worked together for weeks at the Sonoma County Tubbs Fire. During the first night, Uncle Abel and Mr. Dave were literally in the middle of the swirling inferno where hundreds of homes were burned to the ground in a matter of a few hours.

Over time, every month or so, Dave and I would volley back and forth about finally nailing down and committing to doing a show. He just didn't want to pull the trigger. Then in early 2020, I came over with another brainstorming idea. As Dave greeted me, looking like someone had suddenly died, I was almost too afraid to ask. In the guest bedroom there were dozens of stacked boxes. I couldn't believe my ears when Dave told me about his impending divorce. At first it made no sense.

But it was real, and it was happening. Dave had seemed to age twenty years since the last time I had seen him, a couple months prior. His voice was weak and his playful energy zapped. He told me the movers were coming the very next day to take away his wife's things.

I picked up that Dave still called Kay his wife and he still wore his wedding band.

This happy guy had his whole world turned upside down.

Then, days later, COVID hit.

The entire world suddenly came to a stop. It changed everybody's lives, especially for our first responders. But in life, some people falter and some rise to the challenge. Dave stepped in and began recording his podcast.

I learned that fear is stronger than any pandemic. And then there's Dave.

While others were spewing fearful rhetoric, Dave became a quiet, soothing voice of common sense. His audience was starving for this much-needed fatherly comfort in a world going mad. While Dave's world crumbled, he fortified folks' inner spirits to press on and get through the most uncertain and trying times.

More than a year later, Dave finally concluded that he had to move. It killed him again to leave his firefighter family in Sea Ranch.

While proudly serving at two separate fire districts, performing bimonthly podcasts, sadly packing (again), struggling to find a place to live, and assisting with the vaccines, Dave carved out time and gave out thousands of dollars' worth of gift cards to people in his community who were seriously struggling to attain basic needs. It took but a couple of text messages for the whole area to find out that Captain Dave was giving out gift cards!

Grateful, and beyond surprised that someone made them feel valued, my mother texted me about this tall, smiling, blue-eyed man who was giving away money at the local supermarket. Unbeknownst to her, this was my boss, Mr. Pelzer.

In life, it's funny how seemingly small gestures can make the grandest of differences—and when that someone leaves, there's a hole in one's heart.

My uncle Abel, who loved and trusted his friend Dave with his life, once suddenly commented that with Captain Dave's departure, the camaraderie and sense of family within the fire department "evaporated into the wind."

Sometime later I was in the Russian River area. Dave and I scheduled time to go over upcoming shows while he was working on his latest book.

Besides, I wanted to see his new home in the area he yearned for since he was a frightened, lonely, abused child.

In a word, it's spectacular. The home, Dave's home, is as beautiful as it is peaceful.

Although still devastated by so many losses, I could begin to see that Dave was beginning to find inner peace for himself.

To my friend Dave, I say, "For all that you are, all that you've done, and all that you continue to do, God's blessings to you."

FIRE CAPTAIN BRION BORBA

My name is Brion Borba. In my twenty-two years as a professional firefighter, when I think of the dozens of those I have proudly served with, very few stand out for their dedication. One such individual, whom I dubbed "The Man," is Dave Pelzer.

I served as a Captain with Cal Fire at The Sea Ranch Station on the northern coast of California. Cal Fire works alongside The Sea Ranch Volunteer Fire Department, and I heard they had a new firefighter. I first met Dave in the summer of 2013. As with any new firefighter, the spotlight was aimed directly at his head. First impressions can make or break a new firefighter.

My initial size-up of Dave was that he was smart, eager to learn, and extremely witty. Despite how hard I was looking, I could not find any negative attributes to grill him on. I did not know his background, but he seemed well educated. I shook his hand, quickly introduced myself, and we began our weekly drills. Training night ended as fast as it began, and most of the off-duty firefighters went home. I remember Dave sticking around after the drill. I only remember this because he expressed an interest in training beyond that which was required. That is one of the quickest ways to get on a captain's good side. He did not go into much detail about himself, but I could tell he really wanted to become a good firefighter.

As the weeks continued, Dave became a regular around the station. He showed up almost every day. At times before our daily training sessions, I assigned the young firefighters their morning clean up duties. Rather than sit around and have a cup of coffee, Pelzer would immediately jump in and help clean the bathrooms and sweep and mop the floors of the barracks. I've never seen a volunteer do anything like that before.

Dave became such a regular that he would come in and cook elaborate meals for the crew. Cooking is a big thing in the fire department! It's about camaraderie, which in turn builds teams and, more importantly, trust in your firefighter family. Pelzer got it.

It became a tradition that Dave would show up on what was known as "meatloaf Friday." At his own expense, Pelzer doled out sandwiches that were more than six inches thick. It became a dare of sorts of who could actually finish their prized lunch—few did.

Then there was the training. From the, at times, hard-core, to the mundane fire-ground skills. We dragged hose, threw ladders, rescued dummies, used chain saws, practiced rope rescue, and did it all again. Dave's dedication to training was not only good for him; it was good for the whole station. We all became better at our jobs, and it drove home the fact that firefighters are never done training. If you think you are done training in your career, it is time to retire and head out to pasture.

Dave was certainly into it. When challenged, he "threw" a heavy twenty-four-foot ladder, in full gear, including the breathing apparatus. Then he scurried up the ladder while carrying a smaller, fourteen-foot ladder on his right shoulder. Again, I've never seen a volunteer with that zeal.

Still relatively new, Dave took specialty courses like Low Angle Rope Rescue (LARR), which is how we perform critical cliff rescues. If that weren't enough, he also took an intense forty-hour course that included rappelling off towers and moving slabs of concrete after a building collapse. Some of my own firefighters have never taken that class.

We ran many calls together over the next couple of years. He was dependable and he always kept his cool. That is a skill that you cannot teach. Some people have it and some don't. The ability to remain calm in high-stress situations can be more important than any other fire-ground skill. You may be the best firefighter on scene, but if you get worked up and lose your mind, you are going to make mistakes and could get someone hurt. Dave had that sense of calm.

I remember one of those times. We were assigned to clear a fire road east of the station. We were using chain saws to cut fallen trees and widen the road. Halfway through the day, I heard Dave's saw suddenly stop. I looked back to see what he was doing. His nose and face were streaming with blood. A branch he cut was under tension and hit him in the face. He did not even flinch. He asked if his nose was straight and laughed it off. Dave wiped the blood away and kept working. Those are the sort of stories that make a legend.

In 2015, I transferred to Hilton Station near Guerneville, California. I kept in contact with Dave, but we did not see each other as much. That is, until October 8, 2017. After years of extreme drought, California was primed to burn. On the night of October 8, the Diablo Winds (hot and dry offshore winds) began to blow. Sonoma County and other areas of Northern California endured catastrophic wildfires that burned thousands of structures and killed numerous people. One of those fires was the Tubbs Fire. It burned from Calistoga through the hills and into the suburbs of Santa Rosa, well over twenty miles away! The inferno spread to over 36,000 acres in just a few hours. We performed rescues and fought fire all night long.

Late into the next morning, the reality of what took place that night began to set in. My city was burning, and the neighborhood I grew up in was vaporized, reduced to foundations and shells of cars. I had already seen a few victims that didn't make it that morning. The red sky looked apocalyptic. I turned a corner and saw an entire hotel burning. Our battalion chief assigned the two engines from my station to the hotel. On any given day, this would have been a three-alarm fire with multiple engine and truck companies. We only had two. Suddenly, I saw another engine pull up. It was an engine from Sea Ranch. I could not believe who stepped off that engine. It was Dave Pelzer. We fought the fire for hours. I have those memories seared into my brain. It was so amazing to be in that moment, knowing I had seen him as a brand-new firefighter. And now we were working side by side on one of the worst fires I have seen. I knew I didn't need to keep my eye on him. I knew he would use his training and get the job done safely. It was a proud moment and one we didn't even need to acknowledge. The handshake and quick bro hug said it all. Those are the memories that make it all worthwhile.

The Tubbs Fire was not the last fire we fought together. I remember drinking my cup of coffee on a crisp fall morning at the station. The tones went off and we heard the dispatcher announce the magic words, "Structure fire!" We responded and saw the large column of black smoke from the station. We pulled up to the scene and found a two-story house well involved with fire. We took a hose line interior and extinguished the fire on the first floor. As the smoke cleared, I saw my buddy Dave standing next to me. He was off duty, miles away, and returned to Monte Rio, grabbed an engine, and sped to scene. He helped us pull hoses throughout the structure and helped us perform a secondary search. That is a thorough search of the fire building to make sure there are no victims. Much to my surprise, Dave found a victim. The victim appeared green and headless. But as we held our breaths in suspense, the turtle stuck its head out of the shell. We all let out a cheer. Everyone knew this would be one of those fires you remember forever. We saved their house that day, but most importantly, we saved the life of a turtle. It was a momentous day.

One last thing. It may be insignificant to some, but to those of service, most meaningful. At the end of the day, or at shift change, Dave made it a point to shake everyone's hand. Or if someone was having a bad day, a bro hug. He also offered genuine words of encouragement, "Good job. Keep up the good work. Thank you." For the newer, younger seasonal firefighters who were struggling, Dave made it a point to place a firm hand on their shoulders and state, "I'm proud of you. You've got this!"

A simple humane gesture.

That was Dave.

I am blessed that I got to know Dave.

Book Club Questions

Chapter 1
The Deepest of Wells

Have you ever been overwhelmed because of an unexpected event or situation that made you examine your life choices? How did you proceed?

Chapter 2
Damaged Goods

Dave gave advice to a young firefighter to not swallow or bury his feelings—instead, to talk them out. How do you address your challenges?

Chapter 3
Lucky Man

Have you ever experienced an unexpected, life-changing gesture from someone else when you thought you were all alone or forgotten? How did that impact you?

Or have you ever been the recipient of a simple act of kindness? Did that change your outlook or behavior toward others? Do you make it a point to reach out to others with a kind gesture? If so, what has been their response when you do?

Chapter 4
The Odyssey of Sleep

For a time, Dave was unable to sleep because he didn't feel safe. What makes you feel unsafe and what do you do to help yourself feel secure?

Chapter 5
The Long Suffering

How has the pandemic affected you, your job, your family, or your lifestyle? Has it changed your outlook on life and what you value? Did you make any changes because of that? How has it changed your perspective?

Chapter 6
Now Begin

Resilience is the ability to recover from difficulties. Did this chapter give you an understanding of your own resilience? That you can continue no matter what life puts in front of you? What are some obstacles in your life that could have broken you but did not? How did you feel when you pushed past them?

Chapter 7
Turning Points

Think about a time when you were afraid to do something but stepped out of your "protective box" and took a chance despite the odds. Even if it may not have come to fruition, how did it make you feel? Were you proud of the effort?

Did it make you think that you could take on more challenges that you hadn't thought of before this? Are there any other ventures that you may wish to fulfill?

Chapter 8
Time, in Our World

Have you ever kept yourself so busy you did not realize it was affecting and causing problems in your personal life? Have you ever lost a relationship because of this inattention?

Chapter 9
Push Through

What is your "'cause I lived in a basement" moment?

Chapter 10
State of Grace

What is your "Monet painting" moment of seeing something for the first time even though it has been there all along? Did it change your awareness? If so, how?

During the journey through this book, did you discover that those who become consumed with hatred manifest as a virus of sorts that spreads negativity and malice to everyone in their path? Did you also realize that one of the cures to that illness is forgiveness and humanity? How has this affected your life experiences?

About the Cover Artist
Nan Still

NAN STILL has lived along the Russian River since 2008, but she has been painting its beauty for years while spending time at a cabin in Guerneville. Her palette is inspired by the greens of the redwoods, the golds of the vineyards, and the blues of the water. She is a member of the Russian River Art Gallery and her work includes original watercolors, limited edition giclee prints, matted prints and cards, and private commissions. See her work at: https://www.russianrivergallery.com/.

About the Author

DAVE PELZER is a living testament of a self-made man who has dedicated his life to helping others to help themselves. He is the host of the Apple podcast *The Dave Pelzer Show,* which embodies esprit—spirit, humor, and wit—and provides commonsense advice for a more fulfilled life. Through stories of personal experience, Dave commits his absolute best to educate, challenge, and help his listeners to know that no matter the world around them, they are safe within themselves.

He's the author of nine inspirational books. His first book, *A Child Called "It,"* was on the *New York Times* bestsellers list for a record-setting six years. He was the first author to have four #1 international best sellers and to have four books simultaneously on the *New York Times* bestsellers list.

Some of Dave's distinctive accomplishments have been recognized through several prestigious awards, as well as personal commendations from four US presidents. In 1993, Dave was honored as one of the Ten Outstanding Young Americans, joining a distinguished group including John F. Kennedy and Walt Disney. In 1994, Dave was the only American to be honored among The Outstanding Young Persons of the World! In 2005, Dave received the National Jefferson Award, which is considered the Pulitzer Prize of public service.

Unbeknownst to the general public, from 2006 to 2010, while at extreme risk plus using his own time and expense, Dave spent weeks at a time visiting the troops in the Middle East and Southwest Asia, providing counseling and comedic presentations to embedded troops. For nearly a decade, when not on the road speaking, performing radio presentations, or offering counseling services, Dave served his community as a volunteer fire captain for two separate districts. He has served in many explosive fires, floods, and other natural disasters. For his efforts, Dave was twice selected as Volunteer Firefighter of the Year.

Visit www.davepelzer.com or listen to *The Dave Pelzer Show* on Apple Podcasts.

When he is not being of service to others or spending time with his family, Dave lives a quiet life with his tortoise twins (Sneaky Pete and Little Rascal).